5/8/16

Social Issues
in Literature

Violence in
Anthony Burgess's
A Clockwork Orange

Other Books in the Social Issues in Literature Series:

Social Issues
in Literature

Violence in
Anthony Burgess's
A Clockwork Orange

Dedria Bryfonski, Book Editor

GREENHAVEN PRESS
A part of Gale, Cengage Learning

GALE
CENGAGE Learning·

Farmington Hills, Mich • San Francisco • New York • Waterville, Maine
Meriden, Conn • Mason, Ohio • Chicago

GALE
CENGAGE Learning·

Elizabeth Des Chenes, *Director, Content Strategy*
Douglas Dentino, *Manager, New Product*

© 2015 Greenhaven Press, a part of Gale, Cengage Learning

WCN: 01-100-101

Articles in Greenhaven Press anthologies are often edited for length to meet page requirements. In addition, original titles of these works are changed to clearly present the main thesis and to explicitly indicate the author's opinion. Every effort is made to ensure that Greenhaven Press accurately reflects the original intent of the authors. Every effort has been made to trace the owners of copyrighted material.

Cover image © Daily Mail/Rex/Alamy.

LIBRARY OF CONGRESS CATALOGING-IN-PUBLICATION DATA

Violence in Anthony Burgess's A Clockwork Orange / edited by Dedria Bryfonski, book editor.
        pages cm. -- (Social Issues in Literature)
        Summary: "This volume explores the life and work of Anthony Burgess, focusing on themes of human nature, violence, and freedom of choice. Contemporary issues including gang violence and violence against women are also discussed"--Provided by publisher.
        Summary: "This series brings together the disciplines of sociology and literature. It looks at a work of literature through the lens of the major social issue that is reflected in it"-- Provided by publisher.
        Includes bibliographical references and index.
        ISBN 978-0-7377-6988-3 (hardback) -- ISBN 978-0-7377-6989-0 (paperback)
        1. Burgess, Anthony, 1917-1993. Clockwork orange. 2. Violence in literature. I. Bryfonski, Dedria, editor of compilation.
        PR6052.U638C597 2014
        823'.914--dc23
                                                                2014004369

Printed in the United States of America
2 3 4 5 6   20 19 18 17 16

Contents

Chapter 1: Background on Anthony Burgess

The author of approximately sixty books of fiction and literary criticism, Anthony Burgess was one of twentieth-century England's most prolific as well as accomplished writers. Burgess's obsession with violence in his fiction was sparked by a vicious assault on his wife that caused her to lose their unborn child.

Burgess was a larger-than-life presence who wrote prolifically and with elegance, spoke eloquently and dramatically, and possessed an intelligence that ranged over numerous fields. However, underneath the ostentatious façade there existed a gentle man of letters.

Chapter 2: Violence in *A Clockwork Orange*

Responding to critics who complained that the movie *A Clockwork Orange* was too violent, Burgess claims the violence in both the book and movie was necessary to demonstrate the depravity of the life Alex was leading.

Both good and evil must be allowed to exist in the world so that man can exercise his free choice. Without the freedom to choose good or evil, we live in a totalitarian state.

Chapter 3: Contemporary Perspectives on Violence

Introduction

Reading the books of Anthony Burgess serves as a window into his life—for his life history, reflections on his experiences, and the people he encountered supplied the material he mined in writing his more than thirty novels. As his career developed, he became more skillful at disguising people. (An early book, *The Worm and the Ring*, was withdrawn from publication as the result of a libel suit.) *A Clockwork Orange*, Burgess's most celebrated and controversial novel, was inspired by an assault on Burgess's first wife and the experiences from a trip the couple took to Russia.

A Clockwork Orange begins with an account of the activities of a lawless teenage gang as they terrorize a community. The gang leader and narrator of the novel, Alex, is cheerfully amoral as he engages in "ultra-violence"—rape, torture, assault, and finally murder. The novel and later the Stanley Kubrick film based on the novel were highly controversial, both for the graphic nature of the violence and the disquieting portrayal of Alex as seductively charming and wholly evil. Some critics argued that the violence was titillating and gratuitous. In England, Burgess's own country, the film was accused of inciting real-life violence and was withdrawn from circulation. To the charge that *A Clockwork Orange* was responsible for violence, Burgess responded in a 1974 interview for *Un Bellissimo Messaggio*: "If I am responsible for young boys beating up old men or killing old women after having seen the film then Shakespeare is responsible every time some young man decides to kill his uncle and blames it on Hamlet." Burgess also rebutted the charge of glorified violence, stating in an article appearing in the *Listener* in 1972 that "the story of Alex's reclamation would have lost force if we weren't permitted to see what he was being reclaimed from." In the same article, Burgess divulged the brutal inspiration for the violence in the novel, saying, "the depiction of violence was intended as both an act of catharsis and an act of charity, since my own wife was the subject of vicious and mindless violence."

During World War II, Burgess was stationed in Gibraltar as a junior instructor in the Army Education Corps while his first wife, Lynne, remained in London working at the Ministry of War Transport. Leaving the office late one evening in April 1944, the pregnant Lynne was set upon by a group of four men. Although the men were in civilian clothes, Lynne believed them to be former US servicemen, probably deserters. Possessing a feisty temperament, Lynne attempted to resist her attackers. She was beaten and thrown to the ground, where she was kicked, and one man tried to pull off her gold wedding ring, indicating he would break or cut off her finger to get it. As a result of her beating, Lynne miscarried her unborn child.

Following the attack, Lynne developed anemia and her doctors recommended that she drink several pints of iron-rich Guinness a day. She became an alcoholic and eventually succumbed to cirrhosis of the liver in 1968. Burgess blamed the attack for her subsequent illnesses and death. In an interview with C. Robert Jennings in the September 1974 issue of *Playboy* magazine, Burgess said, "[the attack] was followed by a disease that was very hard for the gynecologists to explain. It brought on perpetual loss of blood, perpetual menstruation, so there had to be a corresponding intake of fluid. She was not able to have children or even to have intercourse for a long time. Things never got really right again. And so she just resigned herself to the idea of wanting to die and drank steadily. I couldn't stop her. Finally she got what she wanted."

In the *Un Bellissimo Messaggio* interview, Burgess explained how writing *A Clockwork Orange* was an act of catharsis:

"I think it's the job of the artist, especially the novelist, to take events like that from his own life, or from the lives of those near to him, and to purge them, to cathartise the pain, the anguish, in a work of art.

It's one of the jobs of art. I think it was D.H. Lawrence who said 'We shed our sicknesses in works of art.'

In this sense, the part of the novel, the part of the film, in which the character is writing a book, the book is called in my own book, *A Clockwork Orange*. It was an attempt to put myself in the novel, to put myself as a writer who is subject to the deprivations, to the violence of wild youth, and by that means to clear it out of my system so that I didn't have to think about it anymore."

In 1960 Burgess and Lynne returned from his teaching assignment in Brunei to London, where they witnessed the new phenomenon of teenage gangs. The nattily dressed teddy boys who terrorized the citizenry of London were being replaced by the mods and rockers. Burgess began work on a novel centered on the violence of teenage gangs, but put it aside because he felt the slang of gang members of the 1960s would soon seem dated. On a trip to Leningrad, which is present-day St. Petersburg, in 1962, Burgess encountered the Russian equivalent of teddy boys, called *stilyagi*. Early one morning when the Burgesses were leaving a restaurant, they encountered two rival Russian youth gangs fighting. The gangs politely let the Burgesses through, then resumed their violence. According to biographer Andrew Biswell in *The Real Life of Anthony Burgess*:

"What struck him about this incident was the internationalism of well-dressed, violent youth. To the eye of the novelist, these Russian thugs, dressed in the height of Soviet summer fashion, were indistinguishable from the quaffed, suited, knuckle-duster-wielding counterparts in England. The enactment outside the Metropol of ritualistic, dandified violence provided a solid rationale for Alex and his three droogs."

Struck by the universality of teenage aggression, Burgess began rewriting the book that would become *A Clockwork Orange*, substituting a jargon loosely based on Russian for London teenage slang. Although Burgess would later call the book his least favorite, both *Time* magazine and Modern Library have placed it on their lists of the one hundred best English-language books of the twentieth century.

Chronology

1917

John Anthony Burgess Wilson is born in Harpurhey, Manchester, on February 25, to Elizabeth Burgess and Joseph Wilson.

1918

Burgess's older sister, Muriel, dies of influenza on November 15. His mother succumbs to the same illness four days later. Burgess is sent to live with his maternal aunt, Ann Bromley, in Crumpsall.

1922

Joseph Wilson marries a publican, Margaret Dwyer, and Burgess moves back with his father and stepmother. The family lives above a pub, the Golden Eagle, on Lodge Street in Manchester. A few years later, they move to Moss Side, also in Manchester.

1928

The Wilson family moves to Princess Rd. in Manchester, and Burgess's hated stepmother opens an off-license pub in nearby Moss Lane East.

1928–1937

Burgess attends Xaverian College in Rusholme. His first published poems appear in the school magazine, the *Manchester Xaverian*, under the name John Burgess Wilson.

1937

Burgess enters the University of Manchester in October. Failing to gain a place in the music department, Burgess majors in English literature.

1938

Joseph Wilson dies on April 18.

1940

Burgess graduates from the University of Manchester and is conscripted into the British Army.

1942

Burgess and Llewela Isherwood Jones, known as Lynne, are married at the Register Office in Bournemouth on January 28, while he is on leave from the military.

1943

Burgess is posted to Gibraltar, where he teaches in the Army Education Corps.

1944

In April, Burgess's wife is attacked and beaten by four men and loses the child she is carrying.

1946–1948

Burgess is employed by the Central Advisory Council for adult education by the Ministry of Education.

1948–1950

Burgess is a lecturer in phonetics for the Ministry of Education, Preston, Lancaster.

1950–1954

Burgess is employed at Banbury Grammar School in Oxfordshire.

1954–1957

Burgess is a senior lecturer in English at the Malayan Teachers' Training College in Malaya.

1956

Time for a Tiger, the first novel of *The Malayan Trilogy*, is published in October under the pseudonym Anthony Burgess.

1957–1960

Burgess is an English-language specialist in the education department, Brunei, Borneo.

1958

English Literature: A Survey for Students and *The Enemy in the Blanket*, the second novel of *The Malayan Trilogy*, are published.

1959

Beds in the East, the final novel of *The Malayan Trilogy*, is published. Burgess collapses while teaching in Brunei and returns to England for treatment. Doctors diagnose a brain tumor and tell Burgess it is likely to kill him within a year.

1960

The Right to an Answer and *The Doctor Is Sick* are published.

1961

The first of Burgess's novels using pseudonym Joseph Kell is published as *One Hand Clapping*. *The Worm and the Ring* is published in May. A number of characters in it were drawn from people Burgess met while teaching at Banbury Grammar School, and he found himself accused of libel by the school secretary. *Devil of a State*, a satire based on Burgess's experiences in Brunei, is published in October.

1962

A Clockwork Orange is published in May. *The Wanting Seed*, a dystopian novel, is published in October.

1963

Honey for the Bears, a novel based on a trip to Leningrad undertaken by Burgess and his wife, is published in March. A second novel under the name Joseph Kell, *Inside Mr Enderby*, is published in April.

1964

Nothing Like the Sun, a fictional biography of William Shakespeare, is published in April.

1965

A critical study of James Joyce, *Here Comes Everybody*, is published in September. The first novel he wrote, based on his wartime experiences in Gibraltar, is eventually published as *A Vision of Battlements*.

1966

Tremor of Intent is published.

1968

Burgess's wife, Lynne, dies of liver failure in March. Liana Macellari and Burgess are married on September 9, and they move to Malta with Paulo Andrea, Macellari's son, in November.

1971

M/F is published in June. Stanley Kubrick's film version of *A Clockwork Orange* opens in the United States on December 1. The Burgesses purchase a flat in Rome and a house in nearby Bracciano.

1974

Napoleon Symphony, a novel based on Burgess's work with Stanley Kubrick on a potential film about Napoleon Bonaparte, is published. *The Clockwork Testament* is also published.

1975

Symphony No. 3 in C by Burgess is performed by the University of Iowa Symphony Orchestra. The Burgesses move to Monaco.

1976

Moses, an epic narrative poem, and *A Long Trip to Teatime*, a children's book, are published.

1977

Abba Abba is published.

1978

1985 is published.

1979

A second children's book, *The Land Where the Ice Cream Grows*, and a historical novel, *Man of Nazareth*, are published.

1980

Earthly Powers is published in October.

1982

The End of the World News and *This Man and Music*, a musical autobiography, are published.

1985

Flame into Being, a critical study of D.H. Lawrence, and *The Kingdom of the Wicked* are published. *Oberon Old and New*, a libretto, is performed in Glasgow in October.

1986

Homage to Qwert Yuiop, a collection of Burgess's journalism, and *The Pianoplayers* are published. *Little Wilson and Big God*, the first volume of Burgess's autobiography, is published.

1989

Any Old Iron is published and wins the Portico Prize for Literature in Manchester. *The Devil's Mode*, a collection of short stories, is published in November.

1990

You've Had Your Time, the second volume of Burgess's autobiography, is published.

1991

Mozart and the Wolf Gang is published.

1992

A Mouthful of Air: Language, Languages, Especially English is published in October.

1993

A Dead Man in Deptford, a story about the life and death of Christopher Marlowe, is published in May. Burgess dies of lung cancer on November 22 in London.

1995

Byrne is published posthumously.

Background on
Anthony Burgess

The Life of Anthony Burgess

Geoffrey Aggeler

A professor, literary critic, novelist, and short story writer, Geoffrey Aggeler is professor emeritus of English at the University of Utah and a visiting professor in the writing program and drama department at the University of California at Santa Barbara. He is the author of Anthony Burgess: The Artist as Novelist.

A diagnosis of a brain tumor that would probably end his life within a year was responsible for Anthony Burgess writing five novels in twelve months, according to Aggeler in the following viewpoint. Prior to that time, Burgess had written the novels known as The Malayan Trilogy, *which were moderately successful. With his death sentence, the critic goes on to say, Burgess entered into a period of tremendous productivity to secure posthumous royalties on which his widow would be able to live. When the year had passed, Burgess's health improved, and he continued to be an extraordinarily prolific writer for the rest of his life, Aggeler explains.*

Widely regarded as one of the foremost contemporary fiction writers in English, Anthony Burgess began his long and prolific literary career while living in Malaya during the late 1950s. In 1949 he had written a fictional account of his wartime experiences in Gibraltar, but this work did not appear until 1965 as *A Vision of Battlements*. He started writing fiction during his Malayan years "as a sort of gentlemanly hobby, because I knew there wasn't any money in it." At the time he was an education officer with the British Colonial Service, and the fiction he was writing included realistic portrayals of actual events and personalities. Since it was regarded

Geoffrey Aggeler, "Anthony Burgess," *Dictionary of Literary Biography*, vol. 194, British Novelists Since 1960, Second Series, edited by Merritt Moseley, Detroit: Gale Research, 1998, pp. 51–55, 57–60, 63, 71–72. Copyright © 1998 Cengage Learning.

as indiscreet for one in his position to have such fiction published under his own name, he adopted the nom de plume [pen name] "Anthony Burgess," which consists of his confirmation name and his mother's maiden name. His full name, which he seldom uses, is John Anthony Burgess Wilson.

Music and Catholicism Were Important Influences

Abundantly reflected in Burgess's fiction is his Roman Catholic background, which was part of an ancient regional and family heritage. He came from an old Lancashire family whose Catholic heritage reaches back through centuries. . . . Burgess renounced Catholicism at about age sixteen, but the renunciation gave him little joy. Although intellectually he was convinced that he could be a freethinker, emotionally he was keenly aware of hell and damnation, and to some extent he remained so.

His most persistent youthful ambition was to become a composer, and when he entered the University of Manchester, he wanted to study music. However, lacking the science background required by the music department, he had to take English language and literature instead. . . .

Burgess managed to get through the required courses at Manchester without much effort, but he tended to neglect subjects other than English. The energy he failed to spend on course work he poured into editing the university magazine, *The Serpent,* and into the dramatic society. Unlike many of his contemporaries, who were involved in some form of political activity, he had no interest in politics. The university's socialist society had no more appeal for him than its fascist society, and he maintained, as he has maintained since about age fourteen, a stance neither radical nor conservative nor anything but "just vaguely cynical." This point of view manifests itself in his fictional conflicts between "Pelagians" and "Augustinians." [Pelagians denied the doctrine of original sin and said that people have free choice and thus play a major role in their own salvation. St. Augustine believed in original sin and stated that only with God's grace can individuals be saved.]

While at Manchester he met a Welsh girl, Llewela [Lynne] Isherwood Jones, a distant cousin of Christopher Isherwood. Four years younger than Burgess, she was an economics honors student at the university. They were married in 1942, and the marriage lasted until her death in 1968 after many years of severe illness.

Burgess in the Army

In October 1940 after taking his degree Burgess joined the British Army and was assigned to the Royal Army Medical Corps. He was then sent to join a small entertainment group as a pianist and arranger. The group, all of whose members except Burgess had been professional entertainers, gave concerts at camps and lonely batteries, relieving the boredom of soldiers who were sick of the "phoney war." Then in 1943, having been transferred to the Army Education Corps, he was sent to Gibraltar, where he remained until 1946. The story of Richard Ennis in *A Vision of Battlements* is, he said, "pretty close to my own story." Like Ennis, Burgess lectured to the troops and taught them useful skills, such as map reading and foreign languages. Unlike Ennis, however, he was involved with army intelligence in cipher work. It was a frustrating, dreary time for him. He composed a good deal of music, including a symphony and a concerto, but not much literature.

Burgess's first year on Gibraltar was made especially miserable by the news that his wife was hospitalized in London with severe injuries. She had been assaulted on the street by American GIs, deserters bent on robbery, who had beaten her and caused her to abort the child she was carrying. In time Burgess overcame the consuming rage he had felt initially against all American soldiers, but his horror of the action itself, senseless male violence against a defenseless woman, remained undiminished. Clearly this horror was the inspiration for the most shocking scene in *A Clockwork Orange* (1962), the brutal assault on the writer and his wife, as well as the woman-beating incidents in *The Right to an Answer* (1960).

Burgess Begins Teaching

After his discharge from the army in 1946 Burgess's career oscillated between music and teaching. For a time he was a pianist with a little-known jazz combo in London and did arrangements for Eddie Calvert, "the Man with the Golden Trumpet." Then he became a civilian instructor at an army college of education, a lecturer, in an emergency training college for potential teachers, and finally a senior master in a grammar school in Banbury, Oxfordshire, where he remained for four years.

The situation of grammar school teachers was, as he says, "ghastly beyond belief in those days." Negotiations were going on for a new salary scale, but nothing came of them, and Burgess's salary was so wretched that he found it "increasingly impossible to live." His dismal situation was essentially the same as that of Christopher Howarth in *The Worm and the Ring* (1961). Discouraged and desperate, he kept applying for jobs to better himself. Then one night in a drunken stupor he "quite unconsciously" scrawled out an application for a teaching post in Malaya. He was subsequently offered a post on the staff of a public school for Malays in Kuala Kangsar, Malaya, which he accepted with little hesitation.

Burgess found Malaya a fascinating, indeed fantastic, cultural and linguistic mélange, and he was eager to record what he saw. As a musician his first impulse was to orchestrate it, and he actually composed a symphony in which the different ethnic groups reveal themselves in snatches and strains. But the symphony was not well received, and he sought another medium. The resultant oeuvre, published together as *The Malayan Trilogy* in 1964, may be likened to a symphony or a gi-

Anthony Burgess is the author of thirty-three novels, twenty-five works of nonfiction, two volumes of autobiography, three symphonies, and more than 150 other musical works. © Marvin Lichtner/The LIFE Images Collection/Time & Life Pictures/Getty Images.

ant canvas upon which Burgess has painted portraits representing most of the generic types he knew. . . .

Although Burgess might have become a major novelist without going to Malaya and writing the trilogy, the importance of this experience in his development as a novelist was in many ways analogous to the importance of *Endymion* (1818) in John Keats's development as a poet. His success in capturing so much of the cultural variety of Malaya in an extended piece of fiction seems to have been a tremendous impetus for him toward writing other fiction dealing with other worlds he either knew or imagined. He also had the encouragement of perceptive critics.

Burgess enjoyed his teaching in Malaya in spite of a tendency to clash with administrative superiors. After a quarrel with one headmaster he was assigned to the east coast of Malaya as a senior lecturer in a teacher-training college. Then in 1957 Malaya gained its independence, and the future of British expatriates grew doubtful. Shortly thereafter the Malayan government generously provided each erstwhile colonial with a sum of money and then deported him. Burgess soon found another teaching post in Brunei, Borneo. Despite the favorable reception of his Malayan books, he viewed himself not primarily as a novelist but as a professional teacher who simply wrote novels "as a kind of hobby."

In Borneo, as in Malaya, Burgess refused to join the British colonials in their isolation from the native community. His perfect command of Malay and genuine interest in the people enabled him to mix freely with them, and at the expense of antagonizing his fellow colonial officers he won their trust and respect. This relationship led to an invitation to lead the people's freedom party, which he refused. Even so, rumors about his loyalty began to circulate within the British community, and he was stuck with the appellation "bolshy." The antagonism of his fellows and superiors was further augmented by an incident during a garden party in honor of Prince Philip, who was in Brunei on an official visit. As the prince wandered dutifully from group to group, he inquired casually about local conditions: "Everything all right?" All the dazzled colonials replied appropriately that indeed everything was as it should be—all, that is, except Burgess's fiery Welsh wife, who was rumored to be British socialist Aneurin Bevan's sister. She replied bluntly and insultingly that "things bloody well weren't all right," and that, moreover, the British were largely to blame.

Burgess Receives a Death Sentence

After this episode Burgess's days in Brunei would probably have been few even without the physical breakdown that finally sent him back to England. Not long after the garden party Burgess was giving his students a lecture on phonetics when he, like Edwin Spindrift in *The Doctor Is Sick* (1960), suddenly collapsed on the floor of the classroom. He later suspected that it was "a willed collapse out of sheer boredom and frustration." Whatever the cause, with incredible dispatch he was loaded aboard an airliner for England, where doctors . . . diagnosed his ailment as a brain tumor. The neatness with which he was thereby eliminated as a source of official embarrassment in Borneo led him to guess that his hasty removal had as much to do with his general intransigence and the garden party incident as with his collapse on the classroom floor.

The political situation in Borneo was now among the least of his worries. The existence of the brain tumor had been determined primarily on the basis of a spinal tap, which revealed an excess of protein in the spinal fluid. Other excruciating tests followed. Initially the doctors considered removing the tumor, and Burgess was apprehensive lest "they hit my talent instead of my tumor," but they then decided that removal was impossible. Burgess was told he would probably be dead within the year, but that if he managed to live through the year, he could infer that the prognosis had been excessively pessimistic and that he would survive. His situation was extremely dismal—he had no pension, was unable to get a job, and saw no way of providing for his prospective widow. Fortunately, they had been able to bring a bit of money with them from the Far East. His wife, having graduated in economics from the University of Manchester, was knowledgeable in money matters, and she shrewdly invested on the stock exchange the £1,000 they had taken out of Malaya. The stock exchange was a free organization in those days; she could buy and sell on margins, and in a few years she had doubled, then quadrupled, the original sum. The initial sum enabled them to live through the year, from 1959 into 1960, that Burgess had been told would be his last.

Instead of moping about in self-pitying depression he began writing novels, chiefly to secure posthumous royalties. Surprisingly, he felt more exhilarated than depressed, and his "last year on earth" was one of the most productive he has ever known. Five of his novels were written during this period—*The Doctor Is Sick* (1960), *One Hand Clapping* (1961), *The Worm and the Ring* (1961), *The Wanting Seed* (1962), and *Inside Mr Enderby* (1963). These books include some of his best work, and they were not the only things he wrote. . . .

Burgess Becomes a Prolific Writer

As the novels came out, his health improved steadily, and he began to take on various nonfiction writing chores as well. For a time he was both music critic for *Queen*—a British magazine read in the United States—and drama critic for the *Spectator*. One of the trials of this dual role was being dogged by spies assigned "to see whether I really saw an opera and a play on the same night." He also wrote television scripts, including one on Percy Bysshe Shelley and Lord Byron in Switzerland and another on James Joyce. Other projects included a play written at the request of the Phoenix Theatre, London; another one for the BBC; and still another for Independent TV. In addition he was becoming more and more in demand as a book reviewer, and his average yearly output in reviews alone was estimated by one reporter at 150,000 words. But Burgess was primarily a writer of fiction, and most of his boundless energy during the early 1960s went into the writing of novels. He also wrote some short fiction and, although he found the short story a constricting form, contributed several stories to the *Hudson Review, Argosy, Rutgers Review*, and other journals. He also contributed verse to various periodicals, including the *Transatlantic Review, Arts and Letters*, and the *New York Times*; the latter commissioned him to write a poem on the landing of Apollo 11 [first landing on the moon].

Burgess never, however, remained rooted to his writer's chair. Always restless, he traveled a great deal, and so far as his fiction is concerned one of his most productive trips was a visit to Leningrad in 1961. His purpose in going "was to experience life in Leningrad without benefit of Intourist—i.e., as one of the crowd." Before the trip he spent about six weeks reviving his Russian, acquired during the war; his use of the language enabled him to gain a great deal from the experience. . . .

Burgess's Wife Dies

As time passed and Burgess's "terminal year" receded, he became less worried about his own health but more about his wife's. She had never fully recovered from the injuries she received in 1943, and the years in the Far East had been hard on her. She died in 1968 of portal cirrhosis brought on partly by alcoholism but mainly by years of vitamin deprivation in Malaya and Borneo. Although there was little Burgess could do to ease the pain of her last years, he was still burdened with a strong residue of guilt about her death, and this conflict may be reflected in one of his novels, *Beard's Roman Women* (1976).

Some months after his first wife's death he married a lovely, dark-haired Italian contessa, Liliana [also known as Liana] Macellari, whom he had known for several years. She is a philologist and translator whose works include Italian translations of Thomas Pynchon's *V* (1963) and Lawrence Durrell's *The Alexandria Quartet* (1962). . . .

With their son, Andrea, the Burgesses moved to Malta in 1969, where they lived, between lecture tours and a teaching stint in North Carolina, for nearly two years. They soon found that the island had little to recommend it besides its Mediterranean climate. The repressive rule exercised by a church-dominated government made life exceedingly dreary if not intolerable. Yet during his brief, unhappy residence on the island Burgess managed to produce two books: a biography of Shakespeare and the novel *M/F* (1971), which is set in the United States and a tyrannically ruled Caribbean island called "Castita." The striking resemblance this supposedly chaste little island bears to Malta appears to be more than coincidental.

In 1971 Burgess and his wife purchased a flat in Rome (the flat that appears in *Beard's Roman Women*) and acquired a house in the nearby lakeside town of Bracciano (the house that appears in the conclusion of *M/F*). Between tours and visits abroad they lived alternately in the two residences until 1976. Although they found the atmosphere in Rome a good deal more civilized and bearable than that of Malta, after five years they felt compelled to move again. Italy, Burgess believed, was on the verge of civil war. There was a state of general chaos, prices were rising intolerably, and shortages were becoming more than irksome. In addition there was the omnipresent danger of his son Andrea being kidnapped, since Italians tended to believe that all foreigners, especially foreign writers, are rich and capable of paying high ransoms. To escape these nuisances and threats, Burgess moved his family to Monaco.

Although Burgess had been a professional writer for many years, he still did a considerable amount of teaching. He taught widely in the British Commonwealth and Europe as well as in the United States, where he held several visiting appointments at universities, including Princeton and the City University of New York. . . .

Certain Themes Persist in Burgess's Work

The novels Burgess produced during his "terminal year" exhibit themes that he was to develop again and again—the role and situation of the artist vis-à-vis an impinging world, love and decay in the West, the quest for a darker culture, and his view of history as a perpetual oscillation or "waltz" between "Pelagian" and "Augustinian" phases. . . .

In 1962 what was to become Burgess's most widely read novel, *A Clockwork Orange*, was published. (Even before Stanley Kubrick filmed it in 1971, it was his most popular novel, a fact that did not greatly please Burgess, who valued some of his other works more.). . .

Between 1962 and the end of 1980 Burgess produced fifteen novels. Some of these, such as *The Eve of Saint Venus* (1964), *The Clockwork Testament* (1974), *Beard's Roman Women*, and *Abba Abba* (1977), are rather slight books. The most significant are *Nothing Like the Sun* (1964), *Tremor of Intent* (1966), *Enderby Outside* (1968), *M/F, Napoleon Symphony* (1974), and *Earthly Powers* (1980). . . .

Burgess Was a Major Twentieth-Century Novelist

During his last years Burgess and his wife lived in Monte Carlo and in Lugano, Switzerland. He loved to gamble, and when in Monte Carlo he visited the casinos nightly. He knew the royal family well and frequently strolled with Princess Grace, whose death, he suspected, involved foul play.

Wherever he was living, Burgess continued to work systematically from 10 A.M. to 5 P.M., drinking strong tea, chain-smoking small cigars, and producing a thousand words a day, using a word processor for his journalism and a typewriter for fiction. Even when his health began to fail and he had to return to England, he continued writing. Another novel, *A Dead Man in Deptford*, was completed and published in 1993, the year he died of cancer in London. . . .

Burgess's skill and enjoyment of his craft are evident in his last work, left completed at his death and published in 1995. *Byrne* is written primarily in ottava rima [eight-line verse form], and it chronicles the life of Michael Byrne—Irish composer, painter, and womanizer—and some of his offspring. Burgess's sparkling wit earned praise from critics when the book appeared in America in 1997; one writer for *Kirkus Reviews* called *Byrne* "a swan song like no other, and one of the most delightful books of the decade."

Burgess's stature as one of the major British novelists of the century was recognized by critics at least two decades before his last works appeared, and his later novels did not diminish his importance as a force in English fiction. It should also be noted that he produced a considerable body of criticism. He regularly contributed reviews of new novels and produced book-length studies of various writers intended to be helpful to and increase the critical appreciation of what he called "the average reader." . . .

Burgess was a perceptive, sympathetic critic of the works of other writers, and students of his fiction will find that he frequently illuminates his own work in the process of discussing the works of others.

Obituary: Anthony Burgess

Roger Lewis

Roger Lewis is an academic, biographer, and journalist. He is a fellow at Wolfson College in Oxford, England, and is the author of Anthony Burgess, *a biography of the author.*

Anthony Burgess had two personas—the erudite, garrulous, and cosmopolitan intellectual and the sensitive, somewhat neurotic, man of letters, contends Lewis in the following viewpoint. Lewis argues that although Burgess was a great writer, he never wrote a great book. Novels that approach greatness include Earthly Powers *and* Little Wilson and Big God, *Lewis opines.*

To think of him (as was said of a magnifico like Dr Johnson) is to think of an empire falling. All those big books, reference works, volumes of critical essays, plays, opera librettos, orchestral symphonies, and much else, which tumbled out of his head add up to a resplendent career. Simply in terms of sheer quantity, it is hard to believe it was all done by hand. His personal manner, too, was expansive. With his Roman emperor's hairstyle and countenance, and puffing ostentatiously on a cigarillo, he would hold the floor with impromptu lectures on Malay cuisine, [character Leopold] Bloom's Dublin, how Shakespeare spoke, where to buy shoes in Barcelona, the beauty of Sophia Loren, working for Lew Grade, learning Japanese—anything really, so long as he could throw in colourful words: orchidaceous, pinguid, rebarbative. You would think to yourself, there's nothing this man doesn't know.

He was the most self-dramatising of authors, fully aware that 'Anthony Burgess' was a performance perfected over several decades by John Wilson—the name on the birth certificate (25 February 1917) and on the much-used passport. Burgess was the public role, the baritonal, slightly arrogant columnist and literary pundit, the Monte Carlo citizen fancying himself as the heir of James Joyce. Wilson was the more sensitive, chivalrous reality beneath the swagger: the Manchester boy nervous of fame and riches, who shut himself away in a variety of residences (from Sussex to Switzerland, from Princeton to Provence) and who banged out close on a hundred texts—and there are flashes and sparks of genius in every one of them.

It is perhaps Burgess's memoirs, *Little Wilson and Big God* (1986) and *You've Had Your Time* (1990), which constitute his best novels, his masterpieces. Rather in the style of Roy Campbell's similarly rollicking reminiscence, *Light on a Dark Horse*, Burgess allowed fact to become fantasy. (Some of the real people depicted, army colleagues, for example, or former teachers at Banbury Grammar School, were much put out by the fictional embellishments.) Rowdy, lusty, the book presented the author as a persecuted picaro—with women lining up to bed him, with officialdom going out of its way to thwart him, with the universe, you feel, organised specifically for his disadvantage.

It is a tone (of victimised exasperation) found in the Enderby tetralogy—*Inside Mr Enderby* (1963), *Enderby Outside* (1968), *The Clockwork Testament* (1974), and *Enderby's Dark Lady* (1984)—FX [Frances Xavier] Enderby being another of Burgess's fictional doubles, whose ambition is to be left alone in peace so that he can write. The ambition was realised by Burgess himself in 1960. Invalided home from Malaya and Borneo (with an alcoholic wife), having been a tutor at teacher training colleges since 1954, he was deemed, by his own admission, unemployable (owing to a suspected brain tumour, with a prognosis of 12 months—though that medical fact is open to dispute). So he took to the typewriter, having

Anthony Burgess poses while in Paris, France, during a promotional visit during March of 1989. © Ulf Andersen/Hulton Archive/Getty Images.

dabbled both as a writer and a composer since the end of the war, and he made himself into the first highbrow millionaire since [British playwright and novelist] Somerset Maugham.

It is not too fanciful to say that Wilson did indeed die at the end of the 1950s; thereafter, as the reputation of Anthony Burgess grew, the real man receded, to be usurped, at least on television or in magazine profiles, by a paper man. Even friends started to call him Anthony, or Antonio, but never Tony. Lew Grade once called him Tone Boy. (Another alias, Joseph Kell, did not last.) Being an honorary graduate of Manchester and St Andrews universities, he preferred to be addressed (Johnsonianly) as Dr Burgess. But the people he knew pre-1960 always called him John.

Posterity shall have to decide whether, of the actual novels produced, the ones stemming from the early days are actually the best; that is, when there remained Wilsonian experiences to talk about and transfigure. *A Vision of Battlements* (1965) recalled army days in Gibraltar; *The Long Day Wanes* (1965) was a brilliant and ambitious account of the dying days of Empire; *The Worm and the Ring* (1961) captured perfectly the mood of shagged-out post-war England, the rationing and the rain. It was set in Banbury Grammar School, where Wilson taught before leaving for the East. The real school secretary, deciding she could identify herself in the book, sued for libel. The book was withdrawn and never reissued.

And then there were the first two Enderby books (much coveted by Richard Burton as potential film scripts): They depict the life and times of a poetaster whose muse, for some reason, resided in the latrine. Burgess, never quite recovering from the scene in *Ulysses* where Bloom's bowels are moved, took delight in making parallels between Art and the Body; he saw the division as comic—the brain thinking its thoughts while the body answered back with constipation, disease, lust.

Wilson was a rich source of material, as the later memoirs proved; Burgess was not. When Burgess left England for good in 1968, the cable was cut on the past and on contemporary England—so what could he now find to write about? The answer was science fiction and historical romance; works you could research and make up. *The End of the World News* (1982), for example, prophesied the apocalypse, presented a fable about [Austrian neurologist Sigmund] Freud, and presented lyrics for a musical on [Russian revolutionary Leon] Trotsky. Clever, undoubtedly, but empty-hearted? *Moses* (1976), *Man of Nazareth* (1979) and *The Kingdom of the Wicked* (1985) ambitiously rewrote the Bible: Old Testament, New Testament and Acts of the Apostles, it was all run-of-[Cecil B.] DeMille stuff, spun-off from the lucrative screenplays he had been commissioned to write for Lew Grade, Franco Zeffirelli and Vincenzo Labella. *Napoleon Symphony* (1974), which he said was about Bonaparte, as inspired by Beethoven's *Eroica*, began life as a film project with Stanley Kubrick (to whom it is dedicated)—Kubrick's notorious film of *A Clockwork Orange* (1971) being the one work which gave Burgess his greatest gush of fame.

Napoleon Symphony aimed for brilliance (prose constructed out of music), but was a bit pretentious. *M/F* (1971) was, again, experimental. A story of incest, it was based on the work of Claude Lévi-Strauss and Oedipal myths. Little of this was apparent from the bewildering text itself. When Burgess felt he had better explicate his own ravings (in *This Man and Music*, 1982), the effect was not to deepen our appreciation. On the contrary, *M/F* looked the more stiff and overburdened: a recondite crossword puzzle. But we could see what his ambition was. He wanted to write another *Ulysses*.

I suggest that, if you take his work as a whole, he succeeded. Enderby is his Leopold Bloom (as well as self-caricature). Shakespeare, in *Nothing Like the Sun* (1964), is Stephen Dedalus. His own mother, he once said, 'would be easier to recreate in fiction, relating her to Molly Bloom'. Like Joyce, Burgess had a love affair with language. *A Clockwork*

Orange (1962), like *Finnegans Wake*, invented a whole new language, and Burgess actually dashed off a history of linguistics in *Language Made Plain* (1964). One of his last publications, *A Mouthful of Air* (1992), brought his philological and semantic researches up to date, with chapters on Chinese and tips on translating a Sherlock Holmes story into Malay. *Joysprick* (1973) examined 'the language of James Joyce' and *Here Comes Everybody* (1965) was 'An Introduction to James Joyce for the Ordinary Reader'. These primers remain superb assessments, packed with original interpretation. (Burgess was the last of the scholar-critics not to hold a university post.)

In interviews and in his memoirs, Burgess tried hard to lard his origins as Irish. He was, as he frequently said, a Lancashire Catholic whose grandmother was a Mary Ann Finnegan from Tipperary. Manchester, you'd begin to think, listening to him run on, was but a postal district of Dublin.

The obsession (to put it no lower) with the Joycean genius aside, how much of what Burgess did was self-parody? It wasn't all rarefied word games. He did love the garlicky lowlife: the criminal underworld of *The Doctor Is Sick* (1960), [John] Keats's Rome in *Abba Abba* (1977), the brothel keeper in *The Pianoplayers* (1986), the muddle and mess of travel in *The Coaching Days of England 1750–1850* (1966). He loved the musical and adapted *Cyrano de Bergerac* first as an operetta, then as a straight play for Broadway, where it failed ('because it opened the same week as Watergate'). In 1983, the Royal Shakespeare Company, with Derek Jacobi, had Burgess overhaul his translation, this time to enormous acclaim. (Burgess also supplied the subtitles for Gérard Depardieu's film.) Translations of *Carmen* and *Oberon* for Scottish Opera, any number of movie scripts (never made; they languish in the vault of an Italian bank), versions of Sophocles for a theatre in Minneapolis: these were all ways Burgess attempted to be involved with a community bustle of creativity, whilst remaining in solitude abroad. He spent many years trying to interest Hollywood in a musical comedy about Shakespeare, called *The Bawdy Bard*, with Robert Stephens as Will, Maggie Smith as Anne Hathaway and Peter Ustinov as Ben Jonson. As an idea, that is still simply too good to come true. Just before his death he returned to the Elizabethan era, with a thriller about Christopher Marlowe, called *A Dead Man in Deptford*.

How, then, to sum up his achievement? Though I think Burgess was a great writer who never wrote a single great book, many of his outpourings approach eminence. *Earthly Powers* (1980) must rank among the top 10 novels published since the Second World War, even if it was too craftily a synthesis of his other productions. *Little Wilson and Big God* is brave, boastful, and shames those (like Kingsley Amis) who seem to believe that your reminiscences are to be written left-handed. I, for one, also take delight in his squibs, like *Mozart and the Wolf Gang* (1991)—a mixture of imagined conversation between famous composers, short stories, biography, and a dialogue between two characters called 'Anthony' and 'Burgess'; it is full of vigour, wit, invention and gibberish. Had anybody other than Burgess written it, it would never have been set up in printer's ink.

Long after he needed the money, he used up a lot of energy on hack journalism; he knocked off swiftly remaindered books (such as *On Going to Bed*, 1982, or *Ninety-Nine Novels*, 1984); and who knows what he put into those interred film scripts? His journalism, in fact, is a subject in itself. His lively reviews in the *Observer* and the *Independent*, though generous to younger authors, grew testy when contemplating those who had successfully combined the popular and the lofty, those who had spanned intellectual and best-seller markets: [F] Scott Fitzgerald, [John] Steinbeck, [John] Le Carré, for example. He knew that, somehow, he was in that kind of company, not Joyce's or D.H. Lawrence's.

He moved house and country a good deal—nervously shunting about his residences because he had an aversion to paying any form of tax. He once lived in a Dormobile van and ceaselessly crisscrossed the borders of France, Switzerland and Italy to confound the fiscal authorities. I personally met him on several occasions, when the Inland Revenue allowed him back. He did not strike me as a happy creature; but what if there was any bitterness deep down? He had to be on good terms with his neuroses, otherwise would never have written 2,000 words every day for over 30 years.

At first, in my company, he was the bluff Burgess, scowling and frowning and bragging about a book on Lawrence he had scribbled in three weeks. We went with the late Richard Ellmann around New College, Oxford, and Burgess calculated, from memorial stones, how old the famous alumni were when they died. What did he and Ellmann, the world-renowned James Joyce scholar, talk about? Pension funds, income tax, capital-gains liabilities; hanging on to their loot is what absorbed them.

At the now defunct *Punch*, another time, Burgess endured the garrulous serenades of media folk who had read less of his work than they pretended. He took it well—he knew their game. He started to speak in Russian, or perhaps it was Anglo-Saxon. Then, unheralded, I once received a telegram, instructing me to meet him in a theatre foyer. That time I met John Wilson. He was alone (his voluble second wife left behind in Lugano) and utterly generous, utterly a modest man of letters, happy to sign autographs and chat to students. If I had been working on a book about him, I'd have gone off into the night to rewrite, reconsider. I had suddenly been shown the hidden world of his texts: that beneath the belligerence lay a vulnerable intelligence, for whom language was less a weapon than a defence.

Social Issues
in Literature

CHAPTER 2

Violence in
A Clockwork Orange

The Violence in *A Clockwork Orange* Is Not Gratuitous

Anthony Burgess

Anthony Burgess was a multitalented and prolific British author whose works include novels, biographies, literary criticism, librettos, and screenplays. His best-known work is A Clockwork Orange, *which was adapted as a film by Stanley Kubrick.*

In the following viewpoint, Anthony Burgess reflects on the reasons for the violence in his novel A Clockwork Orange *and in the Stanley Kubrick film based on his book. Both the book and the film demonstrate that a world with violence chosen freely is preferable to a world of conditioned goodness, Burgess explains. To those who call the violence gratuitous, Burgess argues that the violence was necessary to show the horror of the existence Alex was leading.*

I went to see Stanley Kubrick's *A Clockwork Orange* in New York, fighting to get in like everybody else. It was worth the fight, I thought—very much a Kubrick movie, technically brilliant, thoughtful, relevant, poetic, mind-opening. It was possible for me to see the work as a radical remaking of my own novel, not as a mere interpretation, and this—the feeling that it was no impertinence to blazon it as *Stanley Kubrick's Clockwork Orange*—is the best tribute I can pay to the Kubrickian mastery. The fact remains, however, that the film sprang out of a book, and some of the controversy which has begun to attach to the film is controversy in which I, inevitably, feel myself involved. In terms of philosophy and even theology, the Kubrick *Orange* is a fruit from my tree.

Anthony Burgess, "Clockwork Marmalade," *The Listener*, vol. 87, no. 2238, February 17, 1972. Copyright © 1972 by the Estate of Anthony Burgess. All rights reserved. Reproduced by permission.

English actor Malcolm McDowell plays Alex in Stanley Kubrick's 1971 film adaptation of Anthony Burgess's A Clockwork Orange. © Sunset Boulevard/Corbis.

Burgess Set Out to Write About Brainwashing

I wrote *A Clockwork Orange* in 1961, which is a very remote year, and I experience some difficulty in empathising with that long-gone writer who, concerned with making a living, wrote as many as five novels in 14 months. The title is the least difficult thing to explain. In 1945, back from the army, I heard an 80-year-old Cockney in a London pub say that somebody was 'as queer as a clockwork orange'. The 'queer' did not mean homosexual: it meant mad. The phrase intrigued me with its unlikely fusion of demotic and surrealistic. For nearly twenty years I wanted to use it as the title of something. During those twenty years I heard it several times more—in Underground stations, in pubs, in television plays—but always from aged Cockneys, never from the young. It was a traditional trope [figure of speech], and it asked to entitle a work which combined a concern with tradition and a bizarre technique. The opportunity to use it came when I conceived the notion of writing a novel about brainwashing. [James] Joyce's Stephen Dedalus (in *Ulysses*) refers to the world as an 'oblate orange';

man is a microcosm or little world; he is a growth as organic as a fruit, capable of colour, fragrance and sweetness; to meddle with him, condition him, is to turn him into a mechanical creation.

There had been some talk in the British press about the problems of growing criminality. The youth of the late fifties were restless and naughty, dissatisfied with the post-war world, violent and destructive, and they—being more conspicuous than mere old-time crooks and hoods—were what many people meant when they talked about growing criminality. Looking back from a peak of violence, we can see that the British teddy boys [thugs] and mods and rockers were mere tyros [beginners] in the craft of anti-social aggression: nevertheless, they were a portent, and the man in the street was right to be scared. How to deal with them? Prison or reform school made them worse: Why not save the taxpayers' money by subjecting them to an easy course in conditioning, some kind of aversion therapy which should make them associate the act of violence with discomfort, nausea, or even intimations of mortality? Many heads nodded at this proposal (not, at the time, a governmental proposal, but one put out by private though influential theoreticians). Heads still nod at it. On *The [David] Frost Show* it was suggested to me that it might have been a good thing if Adolf Hitler had been forced to undergo aversion therapy, so that the very thought of a new *putsch* or pogrom would make him sick up his cream cakes [throw up].

Hitler was, unfortunately, a human being, and if we could have countenanced the conditioning of one human being we would have to accept it for all. Hitler was a great nuisance, but history has known others disruptive enough to make the state's fingers itch—Christ, [Martin] Luther, [Giordano] Bruno, even D.H. Lawrence. One has to be genuinely philosophical about this, however much one has suffered. I don't know how much free will man really possesses ([Richard] Wagner's Hans Sachs said: *Wir sind ein wenig frei*—'we are a little free'), but I do know that what little he seems to have is too precious to encroach on, however good the intentions of the encroacher may be.

A *Clockwork Orange* Is About the Importance of Free Choice

A *Clockwork Orange* was intended to be a sort of tract, even a sermon, on the importance of the power of choice. My hero or anti-hero, Alex, is very vicious, perhaps even impossibly so, but his viciousness is not the product of genetic or social conditioning: It is his own thing, embarked on in full awareness. Alex is evil, not merely misguided, and in a properly run society such evil as he enacts must be checked and punished. But his evil is a human evil, and we recognise in his deeds of aggression potentialities of our own—worked out for the non-criminal citizen in war, sectional injustice, domestic unkindness, armchair dreams. In three ways Alex is an exemplar of humanity: He is aggressive, he loves beauty, he is a language user. Ironically, his name can be taken to mean 'wordless', though he has plenty of words of his own—invented, group dialect. He has, though, no word to say in the running of his community or the managing of the state: He is, to the state, a mere object, something 'out there' like the moon, though not so passive.

Theologically, evil is not quantifiable. Yet I posit the notion that one act of evil may be greater than another, and that perhaps the ultimate act of evil is dehumanisation, the killing of the soul—which is as much as to say the capacity to choose between good and evil acts. Impose on an individual the capacity to be good and only good, and you kill his soul for, presumably, the sake of social stability. What my, and Kubrick's, parable tries to state is that it is preferable to have a world of violence undertaken in full awareness—violence chosen as an act of will—than a world conditioned to be good or harmless. I recognise that the lesson is already becoming an old-fashioned one. [Behaviorist and psychologist] B.F. Skinner, with his ability to believe that there is something *beyond* freedom and dignity, wants to see the death of autonomous man. He may or may not be right, but in terms of the Judeo-Christian ethic that *A Clockwork Orange* tries to express, he is perpetrating a gross heresy. It seems to me in accordance with the tradition that Western man is not yet ready to jettison, that the area in which human choice is a possibility should be extended, even if one comes up against new angels with swords and banners emblazoned *No*. The wish to diminish free will is, I should think, the sin against the Holy Ghost.

In both film and book, the evil that the state performs in brainwashing Alex is seen spectacularly in its own lack of self-awareness as regards non-ethical values. Alex is fond of [Ludwig van] Beethoven, and he has used the Ninth Symphony as a stimulus to dreams of violence. This has been his choice, but there has been nothing to prevent his choosing to use that music as a mere solace or image of divine order. That, by the time his conditioning starts, he has not yet made the better choice does not mean that he will never do it. But, with an aversion therapy which associates Beethoven and violence, that choice is taken away from him forever. It is an unlooked-for punishment and it is tantamount to robbing a man—stupidly, casually—of his right to enjoy the divine vision. For there is a good beyond mere ethical good, which is always existential: There is the *essential* good, that aspect of God which we can prefigure more in the taste of an apple or the sound of music than in mere right action or even charity.

The Violence Is There for a Reason

What hurts me, as also Kubrick, is the allegation made by some viewers and readers of *A Clockwork Orange* that there is a gratuitous indulgence in violence which turns an intended homiletic work into a pornographic one. It was certainly no pleasure to me to describe acts of violence when writing the novel: I indulged in excess, in caricature, even in an invented dialect with the purpose of making the violence more symbolic than realistic, and Kubrick found remarkable cinematic equivalents for my own literary devices. It would have been pleasanter, and would have made more friends, if there had been no violence at all, but the story of Alex's reclamation would have lost force if we weren't permitted to see what he was being reclaimed from. For my own part, the depiction of violence was intended as both an act of catharsis and an act of charity, since my own wife was the subject of vicious and mindless violence in blacked-out London in 1942, when she was robbed and beaten by three GI deserters. Readers of my book may remember that the author whose wife is raped is the author of a work called *A Clockwork Orange*.

Viewers of the film have been disturbed by the fact that Alex, despite his viciousness, is quite likeable. It has required a deliberate self-administered act of aversion therapy on the part of some to dislike him, and to let righteous indignation get in the way of human charity. The point is that, if we are going to love mankind, we will have to love Alex as a not unrepresentative member of it. The place where Alex and his mirror-image F. Alexander are most guilty of hate and violence is called HOME, and it is here, we are told, that charity ought to begin. But towards that mechanism, the state, which, first, is concerned with self-perpetuation and, second, is happiest when human beings are predictable and controllable, we have no duty at all, certainly no duty of charity.

A Clockwork Orange Warns of the Danger of Misuse of Power

I have a final point to make, and this will not interest many who like to think of Kubrick's *Orange* rather than Burgess's. The language of both movie and book (called Nadsat—the Russian 'teen' suffix as in *pyatnadsat*, meaning fifteen) is no

mere decoration, nor is it a sinister indication of the subliminal power that a Communist super-state may already be exert-
ing on the young. It was meant to turn *A Clockwork Orange*
into, among other things, a brainwashing primer. You read the
book or see the film, and at the end you should find yourself
in possession of a minimal Russian vocabulary—without effort, with surprise. This is the way brainwashing works. I
chose Russian words because they blend better into English
than those of French or even German (which is already a kind
of English, not exotic enough). But the lesson of *Orange* has
nothing to do with the ideology or repressive techniques of
Soviet Russia: It is wholly concerned with what can happen to
any of us in the West, if we do not keep on our guard. If *Orange*, like *1984*, takes its place as one of the salutary literary
warnings—or cinematic warnings—against flabbiness, sloppy
thinking, and overmuch trust in the state, then it will have
done something of value. For my part, I do not like the book
as much as others I have written: I have kept it, till recently, in
an unopened jar—marmalade, a preserve on a shelf, rather
than an orange on a dish. What I would really like to see is a
film of one of my other novels, all of which are singularly un-
aggressive, but I fear that this is too much to hope for. It looks
as though I must go through life as the fountain and origin of
a great film, and as a man who has to insist, against all opposition, that he is the most unviolent creature alive. Just like
Stanley Kubrick.

The Theme of *A Clockwork Orange* Is the Importance of Freedom of Choice

Richard Mathews

Richard Mathews is the Dana Professor of English at the University of Tampa, where he is also director of the University of Tampa Press and Tampa Review. *He has written numerous books on fantasy and science fiction.*

In A Clockwork Orange, *Anthony Burgess returns to one of his persistent themes—the struggle between the forces of good, symbolized by light, and evil, symbolized by darkness—suggests Mathews in the following viewpoint. Both good and evil must be allowed to exist, for without evil there is no freedom of choice, Mathews points out. As part of his cure, Alex is forced to watch violent films, which Burgess uses to call into question the state's role in violence in the media, the critic relates.*

In 1960, back in England, Burgess began a new decade facing his own imminent death. "What's it going to be then, eh?" asks the first sentence of *A Clockwork Orange*. The pressure of time always strongly felt by Burgess, became an even more significant element in his life and mind. Having practically no insurance, no savings, and with his wife having no career of her own, Burgess felt it necessary to leave her at least some financial resources. He began a period of enormous output, working steadily at the typewriter, with ideas, characters and images churning through his mind in extraordinary ways. Within 18 months he had written *six* novels to help support

Richard Mathews, *"A Clockwork Orange," The Clockwork Universe of Anthony Burgess*, The Milford Series: Popular Writers of Today, vol. 19, pp. 36–43. San Bernardino, CA: Borgo Press, 1978. Copyright © 1978 by Richard Mathews. All rights reserved. Reproduced by permission.

his wife during her widowhood. *A Clockwork Orange* was the first published fruit of this new determination. Perhaps his best-known book, both on its own merits and from the Stanley Kubrick film, *Orange* was a radical experiment for Burgess, and a marked departure from his previous fictional techniques. Having shown himself capable of brilliantly constructed traditional novels, Burgess turned to new novelistic subgenres for variety, hoping at the same time to reach a wider audience.

Burgess's Theme Is the Freedom of Choice

The principal character is altogether a different sort of hero. His name is Alex—Alexander. One of the most famous pupils of Aristotle was Alexander the Great, who at sixteen became regent while his father marched against Byzantium. Alexander's razing of Thebes struck terror into all Greece. The Alex of Burgess's novel is 15 at the start of the book, and commands his own terrorizing "army." In fact, the book has two heroes, both of them named Alexander, and they may be seen as opposite Manichean principles [a religious system believing in dualism, where good and evil and light and dark are opposed], though paradoxically they both champion the same thing in the end; like the biblical stories which hover constantly in the background of the book, one becomes Christ while the other seeks to crucify him.

A Clockwork Orange is a masterpiece as both a novel and a film, but the linguistic richness of the book is unsurpassed. The theme is a simple one, yet like most simple but profound themes it has such complexity that it cannot be unequivocally stated. Essentially, Burgess has written another variation on his Manichean dialectic, but the key issue here is freedom of choice. The book suggests that both sides of the dialectic must be allowed to survive, for without them there would be no real choice, and the world would be based on tyranny rather than freedom. The central character, Alex, seems at first to be an unalloyed embodiment of evil, violence, and Thanatos (the death principle). Yet, these traits are combined with a love for great music, which we already know to be a conventional Burgess signal for virtue, youthful vitality, good looks, wit, and a lively linguistic inventiveness. He is our "humble narrator," and since the story is told in the first person, we naturally feel somewhat close and sympathetic to Alex. His wild slang vocabulary is appealing in its novelty and its rhythms, and serves to distance us somewhat from the real horror of the "ultra-violence" he practices, preserving some room for sympathy in the reader.

The Act of Writing Is a Motif in *A Clockwork Orange*

Books and the act of writing are centrally important to the novel, and they amplify the theme of freedom of choice, freedom of expression. The first victim Alex and his gang attack is a reader, a man carrying books from a library. Their second violence is directed against a writer, the second "Alexander" of the book, a man who is working on a manuscript entitled *A Clockwork Orange*. In his first attack on the writer, Alex takes time to read some of the unfinished work aloud: "The attempt to impose upon man, a creature of growth and capable of sweetness, to ooze juicily at the last round the bearded lips of God, to attempt to impose, I say, laws and conditions appropriate to a mechanical creation, against this I raise my sword-pen—" Alex doesn't really fathom this, for he lives in a young physical world, not in the world of ideas. But by the end of the book, things have come full circle. Alex has become a writer; in fact, he is the narrator of the book we are reading, also entitled *A Clockwork Orange*. And the message of Alex's book, like that of Alexander's, is a warning about the dangers of treating the world and all in it as though it were "a mechanical creation."

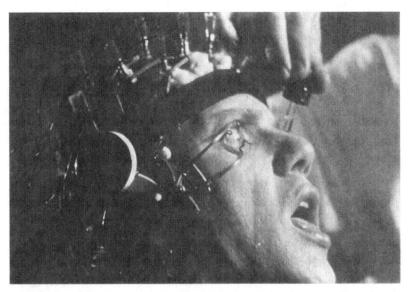

This image from Stanley Kubrick's film adaptation of A Clockwork Orange *shows Alex undergoing the Ludovico technique while in prison.* © AF archive/Alamy.

Alexander later calls Alex a victim of "this modern age," and in a sense he is a kind of victim from the very beginning. Like the other teenagers in this ultra-easy technological world, Alex has been brought up in a Western scientific and mechanistic philosophy which *works* (and like the historical Alexander he is in a sense the pupil of Aristotle, or as one of the other teens mumbles on page three, caught up in "aristotle wishy washy works"). The situation is one we've encountered before—a war without a clearly recognizable enemy: "I couldn't help a bit of disappointment at things as they were in those days," Alex says. "Nothing to fight against really. Everything as easy as kiss-my-sharries." In his clothing and patterns of speech, Alex seems to conform to a teenage contemporary culture, but he departs from them in his solitary appreciation of classical music. The composers he admires are the great German masters—and behind the problems of violence, evil, and the totalitarianism of Alex's gang and the state he lashes out against lie the mixture of great music and tyrannous evil which led Germany into two world wars. After he has beaten and bloodied the writer and his wife, Alex returns to his room and passively listens to classical music while more images of blood and violence race through his brain. He even experiences a passive sexual climax, but just before sleep he says: "I wanted something starry and strong and very firm, so it was J.S. [Johann Sebastian] Bach I had, the Brandenburg Concerto." As he listens to this, he thinks again "on that cottage called HOME. The name was about a clockwork orange. Listening to the J.S. Bach, I began to pony better what that meant now, and I thought, slooshying away to the brown gorgeousness of the starry German master, that I would like to have tolchoked them both harder and ripped them to ribbons on their own floor." Why does the clockwork music of Bach cause Alex to desire even more violence? And particularly, understanding the "Clockwork Orange" manuscript more fully, why is he inclined to rip its author to ribbons?

Alex Is Both Victimizer and Victim

The answer, though never completely clear, seems to be that Alex senses even from the first that *he* is the clockwork orange: He speaks hatefully of himself as "fruit" of his mother's womb because he sees he cannot really change that fact. By implication, he includes us in his circle, addressing us as "brother" and educating us to his slang, and confidentially calling himself "Your Humble Narrator" almost as though he is telling "your" story, our story. He is conscious of himself as writer, and he seems to know what he is doing and he is organizing the book from the very first page, when he speaks of "this evening I'm starting off the story with." When he writes about the problem of evil, of choice, of freedom, he sounds very nearly like a preacher: "But, brothers, this biting of their toe-nails over what is the *cause* of badness is what turns me into a fine laughing malchick. They don't go into what is the cause of *goodness*, so why of the other shop? If lewdies are good that's because they like it, and I wouldn't interfere with their pleasures, and so of the other shop. And I was patronizing the other shop. More, badness is of the self, the one, the you or me on our oddy knockies, and that self is made by old Bog or God and is his great pride and radosty. But the not-self cannot have the bad, meaning they of the government and the judges and the schools cannot allow the bad because they cannot allow the self. And is not our modern history, my brothers, the story of brave malenky selves fighting these big machines? I am serious with you, brothers, over this. But what I do I do because I like to do." In fact having delivered his sermon, Alex reads a priest's message in the newspaper which tends to support his position. The preacher argues "IT WAS THE DEVIL THAT WAS ABROAD and was like ferreting his way into like young and innocent flesh, and it was the adult world that could take the responsibility for this with their wars and bombs and nonsense."

Alex Symbolizes the Solitary Individual

How do you fight an enemy you can't recognize? Is it books, or politics or science which has led us to this state? When the teenage gang attacks they wear masks suggesting a combined enemy: [Benjamin] Disraeli and Henry VIII (politics); Elvis Presley (technology, commercialism and mass culture); and the poet [Percy Bysshe] Shelley (literature). But Alex is a solitary hero, separate from and unlike the crowd he runs with, an individual in the midst of mass society. His own gang turns on him and turns him in for a crime which has resulted in murder. At the end of the first part, consisting of seven chapters (the seven days of creation) he relates: "I was not your handsome young Narrator any longer but a real strack of a sight, my rot swollen and my glazzies all red and my nose bumped a bit also." As they stare at him in the police station he finally admits, "I had become a thing." He finally has been beaten into submission by a clockwork state, "and I thought to myself, Hell and blast you all, if all you bastards are on the side of the Good then I'm glad I belong to the other shop." He observes at the end of the chapter that "my watch having been taken away" he no longer has any idea of the time.

The central group of seven chapters which comprise Part Two provides us our closest view of what the state itself is like in Alex's day. First of all, "going and coming I was 6655321 and not your little droog Alex not on longer." The central question of the book remains the same, and runs like a refrain through the first chapters of this second section: "What's it going to be then, eh?" and the question is part of a sermon being delivered in the jail. The prison chaplain tries to insist that even in imprisonment, the individuals still have a choice. Alex is drawn to the "prison charlie" as he calls him for several reasons. It offers him a fairly comfortable duty, and allows him to listen to "holy music by J. S. Bach and G. F. [George Frideric] Handel" and he even begins to like the Bible: "I read all about the scourging and the crowning with thorns and then the cross veshch and all that cal, and I viddied better that there was something in it. While the stereo played bits of lovely Bach I closed my glazzies and viddied myself helping in and even taking charge of the tolchocking and the nailing in. . . ."

Alex Errs in Trusting the State

But Alex is trapped. In the outside world he seemed condemned to be good, for if he did choose to be bad his freedom would be taken away. In the inside world of the prison, there is even smaller room for choice. The only way out is this brainwashing, and though Alex tries to console himself and the chaplain with his lame remark, "it will be nice to be good, sir," the chaplain replies, "It may be horrible to be good." He continues: "You are passing now to a region where you will be beyond the reach of the power of prayer. A terrible terrible thing to consider. And yet, in a sense, in choosing to be deprived of the ability to make an ethical choice, you have in a sense really chosen the good. So I shall like to think." Alex is moving into a moral and political realm larger than anything he can understand, and we increasingly come to recognize his innocence. In fact, his trust of his fellow gang members had led to his arrest in Part One, and the pattern is repeated as his cell mates blame a murder on him in Part Two. Alex remembers the earlier betrayal as he ponders, "There was no trust anywhere in the world. O my brother, the way I could see it."

Alex does not see things clearly though; he is a member of a generation not allowed to see, but forced to "viddy" and "glazz," and in choosing the Ludovico technique he makes the innocent mistake of trusting the state. His innocence is only accentuated as he ponders the silliness of the officials thinking they can make him good merely by having him watch "sinnys": "I had a real horrorshow smeck at everybody's like innocence." As they wire him into place, he symbolically is subjected precisely to an exaggerated form of the very state treatment he delineated when he complained "There was nothing to fight against really." They make him completely passive, wire him to various machines, inject him with drugs, and force him to watch "A very good like professional piece of sinny." This is essentially the posture the state has adopted for all its inhabitants, forcing them to be dependent upon machines, giving them drugs (the milk bar of the neighborhood tavern), feeding them sinny doses of vicarious excitement. Alex doesn't realize the devastating commentary he makes on society when he innocently observes, "It's funny how the colours of the like real world only seem really real when you viddy them on the screen."

Burgess Questions the Role of Violence in the Media

Burgess raises a very large question about violence in the media. And the painful probing of the question arises even more obviously in Kubrick's violent film. In Burgess's work we are constantly *aware*, of violence as a moral problem. But in much of the professional fare shown in movie houses and on television today (with the approval of the state), the violence is present in detail *without* the moral questioning. Again, Alex is both innocent and acute as he reacts to the films the state makes him watch: "This was real, very real, though if you thought about it properly you couldn't imagine lewdies actually agreeing to having all this done to them in a film, and if these films were made by the Good or the State, you couldn't imagine them being allowed to take these films. . . ." The state is not really concerned with "Good" so much as with Expedient. They will chemically train Alex to be sick at violence without themselves seeking to eliminate the causes of the violence or to strengthen moral understanding. In fact, they have evidently condoned violence in the making of the films, and they are later shown to have purposefully hired the traitorous killers in Alex's former gang as policemen, to conduct regular raids, and beat and maul the citizenry. The violence committed upon Alex by the treatment is that of the mind-snatcher: They so completely rob Alex of choice that he is even afraid of his own sleeping mind, and can only contemplate suicide. By turning Alex even against the music which was his one private pleasure, they make the "innocent" 16-year-old begin to recognize what he is up against: "I don't mind about the ultraviolence and all that cal. I can put up with that. But it's not fair on the music. It's not fair I should feel ill which I'm slooshying lovely Ludwig van [Beethoven] and G. F. Handel and others. All that shows you're an evil lot of bastards and I shall never forgive you, sods." As he says himself, he has become a clockwork orange. Time has run out and has no meaning for him—the state has seized his watch, and with it complete control: "Oh my brothers and friends, it was like an age. It was like the beginning of the world to the end of it." We have come from the Genesis of Part One, through the destruction of Part Two, to "Orange," the omega, the end.

When the prison chaplain witnesses the transformed Alex he continues his objections: "He ceases also to be a creature capable of moral choice"; but the state replies, "These are subtleties. . . . We are not concerned with motive, with the higher ethics." The state is clearly the real author of the clockwork orange, and the Ludovico plan encapsulates and symbolizes the worst features of state control. The Minister of the Inferior, as Alex has appropriately called him, is proud that "it works." The prison charlies sigh, "it works all right, Godhelp the lot of us."

Part Three recapitulates and resolves the themes of the first two parts. The resolution is accomplished not so much in direct action or commentary as in the fact that Alex providentially is led through a number of highly significant returns. He attempts to go back to his parents but finds he has been replaced by a stranger, a lodger, who because he is a stranger and a lodger merely without making the demands of a son, actually suits them better; he is beaten and kicked by the old book-carrying man he had attacked in the first chapter, and this merciless retaliation shows the victim to be no better than the attacker; he is "rescued" by the police, members of his old gang who take him out in the country and beat him to a bloody pulp; and finally, barely conscious and helpless to fight back now that the state has conditioned him, he drags himself to a door he had entered once before at the cottage called "HOME" where the writer Alexander, author of *A Clockwork Orange*, lives. . . .

A Clockwork Orange forces us to examine politics, media, and morality, and to ask what kind of fruit we have grown from "the world-tree in the world-orchard that like Bog or God planted." The action is not so far from the arbitrary violence currently occurring in the large cities of the world. In fact, this is a kind of disorder which has always been with us.

As Alexander puts Alex in an apartment for safe keeping while orchestrating his moves against the political establishment, his friend da Silva tells him: "Rest, rest, perturbed spirit," a remark Hamlet makes to his father's ghost as he discovers something rotten in Denmark. In Shakespeare's play, Hamlet concludes the brief speech by lamenting, "The time is out of joint:—O cursed spite, / That ever I was born to set it right!" Alex is no Hamlet. He is more like the restless ghost who haunts our conscience with his message that our time is out of joint. The clockwork orange state is a rotten mechanical fruit, but on Alex, a ghost who will not be put to rest, Burgess pins the hope that this disturbed spirit may somewhere awaken our sleeping moral sensibilities, that someone will step forth truly to set the time to right.

Burgess Believes It Is Better to Choose Evil than to Have No Choice

A.A. DeVitis

A.A. DeVitis is a professor emeritus at Purdue University and a literary critic.

In A Clockwork Orange, *Anthony Burgess has written a parable about the freedom of choice, explains DeVitis in the following viewpoint. The simple message of this complex novel is that man has freedom of choice and is thus responsible for his actions, the critic contends. Burgess has written a masterful warning of the power of the totalitarian state, if left unchecked, to create programmed automatons.*

In terms of the loosely applied criteria of "black comedy," . . . Anthony Burgess's *A Clockwork Orange* concerns itself with a religious problem: the nature of human will and the importance of individual choice in a socialized and dehumanized world. A drunken prison chaplain says to Alex, the fifteen-year-old protagonist, before he is subjected to the Ludovico process which will force him to choose good at all times: "It may not be nice to be good, little 6655321. It may be horrible to be good. And when I say that to you I realise how self-contradictory that sounds. I know that I shall have many sleepless nights about this. What does God want? Does God want goodness or the choice of goodness? Is a man who chooses the bad perhaps in some way better than the man who has the good imposed upon him. Deep and hard questions. . . ."

A.A. DeVitis, "England, Education, and the Future," *Anthony Burgess*, Twayne's English authors series, pp. 96–118. New York: Twayne, 1972. Copyright © 1983 Cengage Learning.

The England of *A Clockwork Orange* Is a Socialist Nightmare

Alex, the leader of a hoodlum gang and precocious in the ways of evil, can nevertheless appreciate the nature of the choice he makes for evil over good. Together with Georgie, Dim, and Pete, his "droogs," Alex's activities incorporate beatings, robberies, gang wars, rape, and finally murder. Betrayed by his gang after he has forced his way into the home of an old woman who cares for scores of cats and has killed her, Alex is placed in a progressive prison where his education in evil is advanced. His "brainwashing" and his subsequent return to society form the basic plot of the novel and afford Burgess the opportunity to comment hilariously and bitterly about the condition of man in a mechanized world. . . .

Alex's England is a socialized nightmare. People are forced by the government to live regimented lives in blocks of regimented apartments, all the same, all without individuality: "In the hallway was the good old municipal painting on the walls—vecks and ptitsas very well developed, stern in the dignity of labour, at workbench and machine with not one stitch of platties on their well-developed plotts. But of course some of the malchicks living in 18 A had, as was to be expected, embellished and decorated the said big painting with handy pencil and ballpoint, adding hair and stiff rods and dirty ballooning slovos out of the dignified rots of these nagoy (bare, that is) cheenas and vecks."

Music Offers Alex an Escape

Alex's only salvation is music, to which he responds emotionally, ecstatically. To Alex music is "gorgeousness and gorgeosity made flesh" and his reaction to it at first appears mystical in its intensity as well as in its implications, eliciting as it does imagery of a religious nature. But, ironically, the music fails to raise the spirit; for Alex can react only in a physical way to the sounds of the orchestra. For Alex, a creation of the society in which he lives, there are no such things as love, affection, or duty; for only mechanical sex, compliance with the strong, and a display of power mean anything. In other words, Alex is the "clockwork orange" of the title: He is produced by a system, and he exemplifies in his actions the implications of it. He is punished by that same system when his individuality, his love of music, can no longer be ignored by it. Alex is separated from the community not for his evil but because his individuality threatens the status quo. The references to music are introduced to lend a comic as well as ironic perspective to the theme and to afford a unifying factor to the book.

Although Alex's taste in music seems eclectic—he admires modern composers (whose names are invented by Burgess for comic effect) and classical composers as well—it is [Ludwig van] Beethoven whom he most cherishes, and the Ninth Symphony is his favorite composition: "Then I pulled the lovely Ninth out of its sleeve, so that Ludwig Van was not nagoy too, and I set the needle hissing on to the last movement, which was all bliss. There it was then, the bass strings like govoreeting away from under my bed at the rest of the orchestra, and then the male human goloss coming in and telling them all to be joyful, and the lovely blissful tune all about Joy being a glorious spark like of heaven, and then I felt the old tigers leap in me . . . ." Music arouses Alex sexually. At one point he goes into the street, into a record shop, picks up two little girls, gets them drunk on "moloko" (doped milk), and then rapes them, the old "in-out in-out." "Beast and hateful animal. Filthy horror," screams one of the children as she runs from Alex's room. His tigers no longer leaping in him, Alex falls asleep, "with the old Joy Joy Joy crashing and howling away."

In the funniest scene in the novel, Alex and his "droogs" attempt to terrorize the old woman who lives with scores of cats. As he lowers himself from a window into the room, Alex finds himself amidst the cats, their milk saucers, and the terri-

In this image from Stanley Kubrick's 1971 film A Clockwork Orange, *Alex drinks narcotic-laced milk.* © AF archive/Alamy.

fied old woman. To save himself, Alex, as he listens to the screeching symphony of cats and the solo of the old woman, grasps a statue of Beethoven.

Alex Undergoes Brainwashing

Soon after this scene, deserted by his "droogs," Alex finds himself in prison for having caused the death of the "ptitsa." In order to remain near to music, the only relief that Alex has in his prison routine, Alex becomes assistant to the drunken chaplain; and his chief duty is to select and play the recordings used during religious services. When Alex finds himself confronted by evil in the form of a homosexual attack, Alex and his cell mates unite to destroy the pervert; Alex is blamed for the murder.

As a defensive measure designed to check the evil that is threatening the government and causing unrest in the state,

Dr. Brodsky and the minister of the interior, or "Inferior" as Alex refers to him, have devised and sanctioned a process of conditioning human responses closely modeled on [Ivan] Pavlov's experiments with dogs. Alex volunteers for the brainwashing process, feeling that nothing worse can happen to him; but he is mistaken. The process of conditioning, referred to as the "Ludovico process," reminds the reader, of course, of Alex's passion for old Ludwig Van himself. The rehabilitation involves the showing of atrocity films and films of violence, horror, and terror of all kinds. A drug, injected into Alex's system immediately before he witnesses the films, induces nausea; and Alex soon begs to be released from the torment of witnessing the films. His pain becomes so intense that Alex soon discovers that he will do anything to avoid it—indeed, the evil that once had given him such passionate pleasure makes him ill. To do good, even to think good, is the only remedy for the discomfort that has been built into him by the Ludovico process.

Along with the conditioning films that Alex is forced to watch and "appreciate" there are, unfortunately, musical accompaniments; and frequently the music is Beethoven's. Thus the one factor that had set Alex apart from his "droogs," Dim and Georgie and Pete, becomes for him a new measure of pain. If before Alex was a "clockwork orange," subliminally conditioned by his society, now the irony is twofold. Before his brainwashing Alex had chosen, consciously as he thought, the evil action. As a result of his reintegration into a conventionalized society by means of Ludovico processing, Alex is denied choice itself. But, not fully comprehending the extent to which his psyche has been programmed, Alex seeks after his release the ecstasy of a musical binge. Pain and nausea result. To forestall the anguish that results from any confrontation with violence or terror, Alex, who had once reveled in evil, finds himself begging and pleading for everyone's pardon; he has become one of the meek. But the earth is not his to inherit.

At this point the devices of melodrama serve Burgess well, for coincidence and chance unify the activities of the plot. Those very "lewdies" that Alex and his "droogs" had terrorized return to haunt and torment Alex in his newly discovered world of good action. A man who had been attacked while returning home with library books on crystallography sees Alex in the library where he has gone to escape the excruciating torment of piped-in music and exacts his measure of vengeance. When Alex begs for love and forgiveness, he receives instead a terrible beating. Rescued by the police, among whom is Dim, a former "droog," Alex is beaten and is left, covered with blood and half alive, in the country.

Alex Becomes a Puppet of the State

Perhaps the most obvious aspect of the melodramatic plotting concerns F. Alexander, the author of a novel entitled *A Clockwork Orange*. During an evening's escapade, Alex and his "droogs," wearing plastic masks, had forced their way into F. Alexander's house, a place significantly called "HOME," where Alex had remarked the similarity of names. The gang had raped F. Alexander's wife, who had later died as a result of the outrage. It is to the house called "HOME" that Alex once again finds his way. Left by the police, he finds himself befriended by F. Alexander himself. Aware of the irony, Alex for a time forestalls the author's awareness that he, Alex, now a famous personage because of his Ludovico processing, is the same Alex who had invaded the Alexander home earlier on.

Through F. Alexander, Alex is put in communication with the political party attempting to unseat the party that had determined that goodness could be forced upon people. Alex—who becomes a cause, then an issue, in the new political campaign—discovers that once again he is being used; for neither party is at all concerned with his moral emasculation. To serve party interests, Alex is programmed to commit suicide. Rather than endure the constant playing of music mysteriously coming into the locked apartment where he has been placed for his own "safety," Alex jumps from a window. "Friend," says one of the politicians who had coerced Alex, "friend, little friend, the people are on fire with indignation. You have killed those horrible villains' chances of reelection. They will go and will go for ever and ever. You have served Liberty well." But Alex is aware that he has been used; he also realizes that, had he died as a result of the jump, he would have served even better the cause of political expediency.

Either as a result of Alex's fall or as a result of reverse Ludovico processing—the point is never clarified—Alex returns to his old terror-loving, "bolshy" music ways. His final action in the American edition is to return to his "pee" and "em's" house, from which he had been dispossessed by an ersatz son, and to the music of Ludwig Van's Ninth Symphony: "Oh, it was gorgeosity and yumyumyum," writes Alex at the novel's end. "When it came to the Scherzo I could viddy myself very clear running and running on like very light and mysterious nogas, carving the whole litso of the creeching world with my cutthroat britva. And there was the slow movement and the last lovely singing movement still to come. I was cured all right." . . .

Burgess Contends That Governments Create Puppets

In the course of *A Clockwork Orange*'s activities Burgess comments in "black comic" fashion on the horror of life without choice, whether for evil or for good. It is better, he says, to choose evil rather than to be denied the right of choice. Although the direct expression of an orthodox religious code does not figure dominantly within the narrative, the point that moral action and ethical rightness are essential to life in an ordered community is cogently made. Indeed, the final impression that the novel makes is that it is a parable. The point that is left undeveloped concerns the nature of government and the nature of individual responsibility. Burgess forces his reader to come to some logical conclusion, through his "creeching horror-show" scenes, about the choice for right and good action in a civilized community. Frighteningly enough, to choose evil is a privilege that cannot be denied the individual; for, when his choice for evil has been curtailed, his choice of or for good becomes meaningless.

That Alex is as much a "clockwork orange" before as after the Ludovico treatment is ironically and comically portrayed. The sociological implications of the theme are constantly emphasized; and the reader, mystified by the manner and seduced by the virtuosity of the language, at first fails to appreciate the simple homily that man is responsible to himself and to his fellow man.

Burgess, then, in *A Clockwork Orange*, succeeds in garbing a simple thesis in a startlingly telling and darkly humorous disguise. The violence and brutality—the slashing and rapings of the hoodlum gangs, the pack-hunting, the wanton killings—all that Alex represents, all can be found described in today's newspapers. The ultimate terror that Burgess suggests, and what best represents his concern for human beings is that what Alex and his "droogs" symbolize, governments too are involved in, and that depersonalization of family and community life produces "clockwork oranges," that regimentation of human animals into mechanized and orderly units of productive enterprise produces a world without meaning, a world without hope. Symbolically, the world that Alex lives in is one devoid of light and sun; and the majority of scenes take place at night. The people that he lives among are clearly "clockwork oranges," despite the fact that they have not been submitted directly to Ludovico processing.

The Bitter Fruits of Freedom

Robert K. Morris

An educator, book reviewer, and literary critic, Robert K. Morris taught at the City College of New York. He is the author of The Novels of Anthony Powell.

There is no simple answer to the question posed in A Clockwork Orange, *because the question is complex, suggests Morris in the following viewpoint. Burgess asks whether it is better to be an evil human being with free choice, or a "good zombie" with no choice, Morris relates. The critic goes on to say that Burgess leaves the question unanswered while raising the reader's awareness of the inseparable mixture of good and evil in human existence.*

A Clockwork Orange is a book focusing on "the chance to be good" and proceeding from a single, significant existential dilemma: Is an evil human being with free choice preferable to a good zombie without it? Indeed, at two points in the novel Burgess spells out the dilemma for us. On one occasion, Alex, about to submit to conditioning, is admonished by the prison chaplain:

> "It may not be nice to be good, little 6655321. It may be horrible to be good.... Does God want goodness or the choice of goodness? Is a man who chooses the bad perhaps in some ways better than a man who has the good imposed upon him? ... A terrible terrible thing to consider. And yet, in a sense, in choosing to be deprived of the ability to make an ethical choice, you have in a sense really chosen the good."

Robert K. Morris, ed., "The Bitter Fruits of Freedom," reprinted from *The Consolations of Ambiguity: An Essay on the Novels of Anthony Burgess,* pp. 55–75 by permission of the University of Missouri Press. Columbia: University of Missouri Press, 1971. Copyright© 1971 by the Curators of the University of Missouri.

And on the other, the unwitting F. Alexander, with whom Alex finds sanctuary temporarily, similarly remarks:

> "You've sinned, I suppose, but your punishment has been out of all proportion. They have turned you into something other than a human being. You have no power of choice any longer. You are committed to socially acceptable acts, a little machine capable only of good. . . . But the essential intention is the real sin. A man who cannot choose ceases to be a man." (Pp. 153–54)

Yet, were this all Burgess had to say on the matter, the impetus of the dilemma would lose substantially in force. Society at large has never troubled itself with the existential agony (unless to repress some manifestation of it), and judging from the preponderance of sentiment abroad today, it would undoubtedly applaud the conditioning process that champions stability over freedom. But Burgess has found inhering in the central dilemma considerations even more immediate. What distinctions between good and evil are possible in the contemporary world? As absolutes, have such distinctions not been totally perverted or obliterated? And as relative terms, depending for definition on what each negates or excludes, have they not become purely subjective? In a technically perfect society that has sapped our vitality for constructive choice, we are, whether choosing good or evil, zombies of one sort or another: Each of us is a little clockwork orange making up the whole of one great clockwork orange.

I am not suggesting that this spare masterpiece necessarily answers the questions it raises. Even a philosophic novel is fiction before philosophy, a fact too easily lost sight of in the heat of critical exuberance. If anything, Burgess sharpens our sensibilities, shapes our awareness of his main argument, by letting us see the extent to which the human quotient dwindles in the face of philosophic divisions. One must, therefore, reject equally any monistic [a philosophy stating everything can be explained by a single concept] or dualistic readings of the novel, not because the book, per se, is complex, but because the issues are. It is obviously impossible to resolve syllogistically [deductively] which is the greater evil perpetrated in *A Clockwork Orange*: Alex's rape and murder or the state's conditioning of his mind and, as some would have it, soul. Passive goodness and dynamic evil are choices that in themselves may or may not be acceptable or unacceptable, but that in terms of the novel are neither. My own preference is to view the book pluralistically, to see it as a kind of varieties of existential experience, involving at every turn mixtures of both good and evil that move outward through widening concentric circles of choice from the esthetic (ugliness, beauty) to the moral (sin, redemption). And, as with *The Wanting Seed*, the experiences are empirically stated.

Let me start with the esthetic that is oddly integral to the novel—its language. *Vesch* and *tolchock* and *smeck* and about 250 other nadsat neologisms [newly coined words] characterize Alex's era as distinctively as *phony* and *crap* do Holden Caulfield's [in J.D. Salinger's *The Catcher in the Rye*]. Whatever sources Burgess drew upon ("Odd bits of old rhyming slang.... A bit of gypsy talk, too. But most of the roots are Slav. Propaganda. Subliminal penetration."), it has generally been the brutality, harshness, distortion, artificiality, and synthetic quality of the coinages that have fascinated those (myself included) who make the direct connection between the way Alex speaks and how he acts. The language is all of this—an "objective correlative" with a vengeance—but it is something more. Burgess is also a musician, and any passage of sustained nadsat reflects certain rhythms and textures and syncopations. As the following:

> Oh, it was gorgeosity and yumyumyum. When it came to the Scherzo I could viddy myself very clear running and running on like very light and mysterious nogas, carving the whole litso of the creeching world with my cutthroat britva.

> And there was the slow movement and the lovely last sing-
> ing movement still to come. I was cured all right.

In its simplicity and naturalness as well as its wholeness
and continuity, this final paragraph of *A Clockwork Orange*
sings to me much as those freewheeling lapses in Molly
Bloom's soliloquy [in James Joyce's *Ulysses*]. It is hardly coincidental that Alex's favorite piece of music is [Ludwig van]
Beethoven's Ninth [Symphony], rich in dissonances that only
the professional ear can detect, but filled also with as many
untapped, infinite (so it seems) harmonies. In a way it is easy
to understand why musical conservatives of Beethoven's time
could find the Ninth "ugly" by the then rigorous harmonic
standards and why, as a matter of fact, more than one critic
fled from the concert hall at the beginning of the "lovely last
singing movement." Alex's language is, in its way, ugly, too;
but place it alongside the bland and vapid professional or ev-
eryday language of the doctors and warders and chaplains and
hear how hollow their language rings. Burgess was out to
show how sterile and devitalized language could become without a continuing dynamics behind it; how, in fact, the juice
had been squeezed from it; and how, contrarily, Alex emerges
as something of a poet, singing dithyrambs to violence, but
revealing through the terrifying beauty of his speech the naked beauty of an uninhibited psyche.

The choice of an esthetic substantiates the several existential modes without explaining how the maladjustment—itself
an indication of social, psychological, and biological "evils"—
came about. The causes are naturally grounded in current
events, and Burgess has spelled them out in earlier writings.
Alex, the gross product of welfare state overkill, is not "depraved because he is deprived" but because he is indulged.
"Myself," he notes rather pathetically at the beginning of *A
Clockwork Orange*, "I couldn't help a bit of disappointment at
things as they were those days. Nothing to fight against really.
Everything as easy as kiss-my-sharries." Alex's utopia is more

than the result of supra-permissiveness and self-gratification; it is the consequence of the "original sin" inborn with every offspring of modern organizational leviathans. Having discovered that existence has always meant freedom, but never having been taught "goodness," Alex responds predictably and inevitably to the killing burden of choice.

Socially, he and his "droogs" parody the formless, shadowy, omnipotent political entity that sports with them as they with "lewdies." This [Franz] Kafkaesque infinite regression is frightening enough, though I find even more so Burgess' repeated inferences that we are all, in some way or another, products of conditioning: tools to be manipulated and clockwork oranges whether we will or no. Alex, not unlike Meursault or K. [characters in Albert Camus's *The Stranger* and Franz Kafka's *The Trial*] or—as Burgess more slyly than reasonably lets us imagine—Christ, is the mere scapegoat. He is the one called upon to expiate for the existence of others because he has dared question—or (in this case) has been forced to question—his own.

I don't know that Burgess offers any clear-cut expansion of the psychological and biological evils of modern life, but he does dramatize with vitality the theory that we are by now— depending on our luck—either neurotic or paranoid. Alex's particular routine sado-masochism—nightly orgies of "tolchocking" and the old "in-out in-out," alternating between sabbaticals at the all-too-[Sigmund] Freudian Korova Milkbar and withdrawals (onanistic [relating to masturbation] and otherwise) into his multi-speakered stereo womb—may be the healthy neurosis standing between Alex and the paranoia of the populace, though it proves something of a disaster for those elected as outlets for his self-expression. Yet more insidious is the growing feeling one gets in reading *A Clockwork Orange* of governments encouraging violence in order to whip up and feed the paranoia that will ultimately engender allegiance through fear. Ironically, Alex, on the surface at least, is less psychologically distorted and biologically frustrated in his career of violence than those he terrorizes or those who seek to condition him. And, in a more significant way, his small-scale brutalities reflect no deeper abnormality than those of larger scale perfected by the engineers of power politics.

Alex, of course, does not intellectualize his *Non serviam* [Latin for "I will not serve"]. For one thing, he wouldn't know how to; for another, there is no need to. The evils of intel-lect—ignorance and error—have brought the state, to a point at which only the fruits of escalated intellectual achievement can check and contain (if that is now the sole function left the state!) the robots it has brought into being. Nothing is mysti-fying about our present disenchantment with intellectuals who, however motivated or why, have skillfully and near to-tally excised with their finely honed organizations, systems, and machines the last vestiges of our intuition. Burgess makes a case for the Alex-breed being one of the last, though obvi-ously not impregnable, strongholds of intuition. Yet Alex is neither a purely feeling (if ignoble) savage nor a crusader war-ring against thought. He is a prototype of those who, mud-dling means and ends by lumping them together, rebel out of a studied defiance to intellect, rather than out of any untu-tored intuitive urge. Intellect having failed to show them the "truth that shall make men free," intuition alone must sustain the illusion of freedom and itself become accepted as the cre-ative act or be confused with it. Such intuitional virtues seem to account for Alex's successful "dratsing" with Georgie and Dim:

> ... when we got into the street I viddied that thinking is for the gloopy ones and that the oomny ones use like inspira-tion and what Bog sends. For now it was lovely music that came to my aid. There was an auto ittying by and it had its radio on, and I could just slooshy a bar or so of Ludwig Van (it was the Violin Concerto, last movement), and I viddied right at once what to do.

What Alex does is carve up both of them a bit with his "britva," yet the episode is more significant in retrospect than in context. Alex's *natural* reflex of elation in the face of violence—inspired here by Beethoven—later becomes a *conditioned* reflex against violence after his bout with the "Ludovico technique," a name, I imagine, not chosen at random by Burgess. The distortion of intellect and intuition leads to an unresolvable Manicheanism [an ancient religion based on the struggle between good and evil, symbolized by darkness and light]: What are we, where are we when we can be programmed into calling evil what is so clearly the "good and beautiful?" In a clockwork orange society we may as well surrender any pretense for distinguishing between good and evil; when we call them by the identical name we know we have been brainwashed past hope. In this respect, *A Clockwork Orange* shows refinements even beyond [George Orwell's] *1984*. Winston Smith, having undergone physical tortures on a par with primitive atrocities and unrelenting mental cruelties predicated on external fears, quite naturally betrays the woman he loves and learns to love Big Brother. But Alex, robbed of his will, reduced to an automaton, taught to be sickened by violence, is made "good" only by killing in him what was already *the* good.

Both Winston and Alex "die" when they can no longer love. Yet, if *1984* is grimly conclusive in showing the death of a mind and heart at the hands of the state, *A Clockwork Orange* is equally effective in questioning the finality of the death. Burgess brings in (not for shock tactics alone) one of the original archetypes through which Alex finds salvation: the fall, or in this case, the jump. His attempted suicide is, according to Christian dogma, a transgression against God's will, grace, and judgment, and, existentially, the inexcusable surrender of human freedom. Alex, in other words, has been half-dragged, half-propelled down paths of problematical and actual evil to arrive at the lethal nadir of moral evil: sin. And having plumbed the depths, he can only rise. He is a slave to fate rather than choice (the things that happen to him in the last third of the book recapitulate those he initiated in the first third), a victim (no longer victimizer) without refuge, unsuited for Christ-like martyrdom ("If that veck had stayed I might even have like presented the other cheek"), physically coming apart at the seams and mentally wracked. From this condition, his try at "snuffing it" becomes the last desperate exertion of a murdered will and, paradoxically, the means to its resurrection.

Despite the unanswerable paradoxes and dilemmas of *A Clockwork Orange*, which remain unaltered in the ambiguity of its conclusion, my own notions as to the book's ultimate intent are perhaps slightly more irreverent than ambivalent. I cannot escape the idea that Burgess has intended Alex's sickness—the *nausée* lodged in nonchoice—to symbolize a new concept of *Angst* neatly antithetical to [Søren] Kierkegaard's "sickness unto death," the "fear and trembling" accruing from the infinite possibilities of choice. And, further, I suspect Alex's jump, the fall by which he is redeemed (the resulting concussion undoes his conditioning), in some way approximates the Kierkegaardian "leap into faith": the intuitive passage from doubt to faith after the cold logic of intellect fails. Alex has done wrong, been evil, sinned, but all as preparation for his redemption. The faith he finds is a specimen of love, joy, freedom. Ironically, he must leave HOME in order to reach it in the same way a man must "lose his life [before] he saves it." And his cure is both of the body and soul. "It was," says Alex, "like as though to get better I had to get worse." Burgess seems to be saying that, in a brutal, resigned, mechanical world—a world turned clockwork—love must come from hate, good from evil, peace from violence, and redemption from sin.

How? Unfortunately there are no panaceas for metaphysical or existential ills, and Burgess is not a prescriptive writer anyway. Human problems are inexhaustible so long as there are human beings; eradicate one and you eradicate the other. Short of that, one might find the answer to *A Clockwork Orange* in *The Wanting Seed*—and vice versa, but I very much doubt that either solution would serve for long. Give man unlimited choice? He will make a botch of it. Deprive him of all but the "right" choice? He is no longer a man. The seeds and fruits of freedom, both novels tell us, are bitter, but man is now harvesting only what he has sown.

Anthony Burgess's Clockwork Oranges

Stanley Edgar Hyman

An educator and literary critic, Stanley Edgar Hyman was for many years a staff writer on the New Yorker *and served as literary critic for the* New Leader. *He taught at Bennington College and was the author of several works of literary criticism, including* The Armed Vision: A Study in the Methods of Modern Literary Criticism.

Hyman describes the violence in A Clockwork Orange *as both savage and surreal in the following viewpoint. Burgess paints a nightmarish picture of life in socialist England to create a moral fable, Hyman suggests. The book's ultimate irony is that Alex was not made into a "clockwork orange," or zombie, by his brainwashing; he always was preconditioned by the actions of a socialist state.*

Anthony Burgess is one of the newest and most talented of the younger British writers. Although he is 45, he has devoted himself to writing only in the last few years. Before that he was a composer, and a civil servant in Malaya and Brunei. His first novel, *The Right to an Answer*, was published in England in 1960 and here in 1961. It was followed the next year by *Devil of a State*, and now by *A Clockwork Orange*. Burgess seems to me the ablest satirist to appear since Evelyn Waugh, and the word "satire" grows increasingly inadequate to his range.

The Right to an Answer is a terribly funny, terribly bitter smack at English life in a provincial city (apparently the

Stanley Edgar Hyman, "Anthony Burgess' Clockwork Oranges," *The New Leader*, vol. 46, no. 1, January 7, 1963, pp. 22–23. Copyright © 1963 by The New Leader. All rights reserved. Reproduced by permission.

author's birthplace, Manchester). The principal activity of the townspeople seems to be the weekend exchange of wives, and their dispirited slogan is "Bit of fun" (prophetically heard by Mr. Raj, a visiting Ceylonese, as "bitter fun"). The book's ironic message is love. It ends quoting Raj's unfinished manuscript on race relations: "Love seems inevitable, necessary, as normal and as easy a process as respiration, but unfortunately"—the manuscript breaks off. Raj's love has just led him to kill two people and blow his brains out. One thinks of *A Passage to India*, several decades more sour.

Devil of a State is less bitter, more like early Waugh. Its comic target is the uranium-rich East African state of Dunia (obviously based on the oil-rich Borneo state of Brunei). In what there is of a plot, the miserable protagonist, Frank Lydgate, a civil servant, struggles with the rival claims of his wife and his native mistress, only to be snatched from both of them by his first wife, a formidable female spider. The humor derives mostly from incongruity: the staple food in Dunia is Chinese spaghetti; the headhunters upriver shrink a Belgian head with eyeglasses and put Brylcreem on its hair.

Neither book at all prepares one for the savagery of Burgess' new novel. *A Clockwork Orange* is a nightmarish fantasy of a future England where the hoodlums take over after dark. Its subject is the dubious redemption of one such hoodlum, Alex, told by himself. The society is a limp and listless socialism at some future time when men are on the moon. Hardly anyone still reads, although streets are named Amis Avenue and Priestley Place; Jonny Zhivago, a "Russky" pop singer, is a juke-box hit, and the teenage language sounds very Russian; everybody "not a child nor with child nor ill" must work; criminals have to be rehabilitated because all the prison space will soon be needed for politicals; there is an opposition and elections, but they re-elect the government.

The endless sadistic violence in the book, unimaginably nasty, mindless and mind-hating, is described by Alex with eloquence and joy, at least until it turns on him. In the opening pages, we see 15-year-old Alex and the three other boys in his gang out for an evening of fun: They catch an old man carrying library books on the street, beat and kick him bloody, smash his false teeth and tear up his books; then, wearing masks (of Disraeli, Elvis Presley, Henry VIII and Shelley), they rob a shop, beating the middle-aged proprietor and his wife unconscious and undressing the woman for laughs; then they catch another gang raping a child and fight them, chaining one boy in the eyeballs and kicking him unconscious, carving another's face with a razor; they cap off the evening by stealing a car for the "real kick," "the old surprise visit," which consists of invading the suburban house of a writer, tearing up his manuscript, beating him bloody, holding him while they strip his wife and rape her in turn, then smashing up the furniture and urinating in the fireplace; finally they push the car into a filthy canal and go happily home to bed.

The next day Alex pleads a headache and stays home from school. He goes out, picks up two 10-year-old girls, gets them drunk on whisky, injects himself with dope, puts the last movement of Beethoven's Ninth on the phonograph, and rapes both girls, brutally and perversely. That night he fights two members of his gang for leadership and defeats them by cutting their wrists with his razor. It is his high point. The gang then does a burglary job, at which Alex beats an old lady to death. As he flees, with the police coming, one of the boys whose wrist he had cut blinds Alex by chaining him in the eyeballs, and the police catch him.

A streak of grotesque surrealism runs all through Burgess' books. By *A Clockwork Orange* it has become truly infernal. As the hoodlums drive to their "surprise visit," they run over a big snarling toothy thing that screams and squelches, and as they drive back they run over "odd squealing things" all the way.

Alex has no interest in women except as objects of violence and rape (the term for the sex act in his vocabulary is characteristically mechanical, "the old in-out in-out"). No part of the female body is ever mentioned except the size of the breasts (it would also interest a Freudian to know that the hoodlums' drink is doped milk). Alex's only "aesthetic" interest is his passion for symphonic music. He lies naked on his bed, surrounded by his stereo speakers, listening to Mozart or Bach while he daydreams of grinding his boot into the faces of men, or raping ripped screaming girls, and at the music's climax he has an orgasm.

After his capture, Alex is treated as brutally by the police as he treats his victims. In jail, he kicks a cell mate to death, and his reward is being chosen as the first experiment in conditioned reflex rehabilitation. For two weeks he is injected daily with a drug and shown films of sadistic violence even more horrible than his own, accompanied by symphonic music. At the end of that time he is so conditioned that the thought of doing any violence makes him desperately ill, as does the sound of music. In a public display of his cure, he tries to lick the boots of a man hurting him, and he reacts to a beautiful underdressed girl by offering to be her true knight.

It is a moral fable, if a nasty one, and it proceeds with all the patness of moral fable. Eventually Alex tries to kill himself by jumping out a window, and as a result of his new injuries he recovers from the conditioning, and again loves violence and music. He is, he says, "cured."

A running lecture on free will, first from the prison chaplain, then from the writer, strongly suggests that the book's intention is Christian. Deprived of his capacity for moral choice by science, Burgess appears to be saying, Alex is only a "clockwork orange," something mechanical that appears organic. Free to will, even if he wills to sin, Alex is capable of salvation. But perhaps this is to confine Burgess' ironies and ambiguities

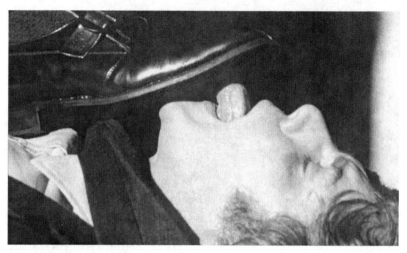

This image from Stanley Kubrick's film adaptation of A Clockwork Orange *shows Alex licking the boot of a man who insults and beats him after he has been transformed from a violent teenager to a "good" citizen.* © Sunset Boulevard/Corbis.

within simple orthodoxy. Alex always *was* a clockwork orange, a machine for mechanical violence far below the level of choice, and his dreary socialist England is a giant clockwork orange.

Perhaps the most fascinating thing about the book is its language. Alex thinks and talks in the "nadsat" (teenage) vocabulary of the future, a remarkable invention by Burgess of several hundred words. It is not quite so hard to decipher as Cretan Linear B, and Alex translates some of it. I found that I could not read the book without compiling a glossary, although some of my translations are approximate. At first the vocabulary seems incomprehensible: "you could peet it with vellocet or synthemesc or drencrom or one or two other veshches." Then the reader discovers that some of it is clear from the context: "to tolchock some old veck in an alley and viddy him swim in his blood." Other words are intelligible after a second context: When Alex kicks an enemy on the "gulliver" it might be any part of the body, but when a glass of beer is served with a gulliver, "gulliver" is "head."

Some of the words are inevitable associations, like "cancer" for "cigarette" or "charlie" for "chapl[a]in," and may even be current English slang. Others are produced simply by schoolboy transformations: "appy polly loggy" (apology), "eggiweg" (egg), "interessovat" (to interest), "skolliwoll" (school). Still others are foreign words slightly distorted: Russian "baboochka" (old woman) and "bolshy" (enormous), Latin "biblio" (library), Chinese "chai" (tea), Italian "gazetta" (newspaper), German "forella" ("trout" as slang for a woman) and "knopka" (button), Yiddish "keeshkas" (guts) and "yahoodies" (Jews), French "sabog" (shoe) and "vaysay" (WC, watercloset).

Other words are onomatopoetic sound imitations: "collocoll" (bell), "razrez" (to tear), "toofles" (slippers). Still others are rhyming slang: "luscious glory" for "hair" (rhyming with "upper story"?) and "pretty polly" for "money" (rhyming with "lolly" of current slang). A few simply distort the word: "banda" (band), "gruppa" (group), "kot" (cat), "minoota" (minute). Others are amputations: "creech" (from "screech"; shout or scream), "domy" (domicile), "guff" (guffaw), "pee and em" (pater and mater), "sarky" (sarcastic), "sinny" (cinema). Some are portmanteau words: "chumble" (chattermumble), "mounch" (mouth-munch), "shive" (shiv-shave), "skriking" (scratching-striking).

The best of them are images and metaphors, some quite imaginative and poetic: "glazz" (eye), "horrorshow" (beautiful, beautifully), "lewdies" (squares), "pan-handle" (erection), "rabbit" (to work), "sammy" (generous, from "Uncle Sam"?), "soviet" (an order), "starry" (ancient), "viddy" (to see, from "video"), "yahzick" (tongue, from "say-*ah*-when-*zick*").

There are slight inconsistencies, when Burgess (or Alex) forgets his word and invents another or uses our word, but on the whole he handles his amazing vocabulary in a masterly fashion. It has a wonderful sound, particularly in abuse, when "grahzny bratchny" sounds infinitely better than "dirty bastard." Coming to literature by way of music, Burgess has a superb ear, and he shows an interest in the texture of language rare among current novelists. As a most promising writer of the '60s, Anthony Burgess has followed novels that remind us of [English novelist E.M.] Forster and Waugh with an eloquent and shocking novel that is quite unique.

An Inhumane Society Both Causes and Fails to Cure Violent Behavior

Thomas Reed Whissen

Thomas Reed Whissen is a professor of English at Wright State University and a literary critic.

One of the major reasons that A Clockwork Orange *became a cult classic is that its highly stylized depiction of a generation gap appealed to the youth of the 1960s and 1970s who were rebelling against an earlier generation, Whissen contends. Many readers believe Burgess blames society for the evils described in the book—a position that cult followers favor.*

On the surface *A Clockwork Orange* is a novel about juvenile delinquents in a near-future Britain, but on a deeper level it is a novel about conditioning and free will. The "clockwork orange" is a metaphor for that fantasy of modern science, the perfectly programmed man. Stanley Kubrick, who had already made Arthur Clarke's *2001: A Space Odyssey* a cult film classic in 1968, did much the same thing for *A Clockwork Orange* when he adapted it into a highly successful film in 1971. Dispute continues over whether this is a cult film or a cult book, but the question is really moot. What matters is that Anthony Burgess's basic concept, by either means, became a definite cult favorite.

A Novel About the Generation Gap

What partially accounts for the popularity of *A Clockwork Orange* as cult fiction is its highly imaginative representation of the generation gap, an expression that had been given new

Thomas Reed Whissen, *"A Clockwork Orange," Classic Cult Fiction: A Companion to Popular Cult Literature*, pp. 62–67. Westport, CT: Greenwood, 1992. Copyright © 1992 by ABC-CLIO. All rights reserved. Reproduced by permission.

meaning by the seemingly unbreachable rift that had divided parents and children into hostile camps by the early seventies. On the one side stood parents, all of whom had experienced in varying degrees of severity the deprivations of the Great Depression and the horrors of World War II. They looked upon themselves as proud survivors and were wont to parade the virtues of asceticism before their spoiled and ungrateful children. On the other side were the children who felt bullied by all the stories of suffering and sacrifice, who felt they were being told that they could never measure up, that no experience of theirs could ever compare with the Depression and the war, that anything that happened to them would pale by comparison. When at last they had heard enough about "making do" and "doing without," about "pitching in" and "muddling through," when they thought they would scream if they heard one more Glenn Miller record or one more comment about how "they don't make 'em like that anymore," they rebelled.

Sick of the Depression, sick of the war, sick of big bands and crew cuts and Peter Pan collars, they turned their backs on the past, despised on principle anything that happened before Elvis [Presley], and set about systematically driving their parents crazy. It was easy. All they had to do was follow one simple principle: If it bugs 'em, do it. Thus, when parents tried to reason with their children, they continued to miss the point. They never saw that their children took the opposite point of view only because it *was* opposite, that they would never give in simply because they were determined not to, regardless of what they might think privately.

When parents pointed to Nazi Germany as an evil enemy, their children spelled America "Amerika" and pointed to the way the United States was treating minorities and third world nations. When parents boasted of winning a war, their children made it a matter of honor to lose one. When parents derided their former enemies, Germany and Japan, their chil-

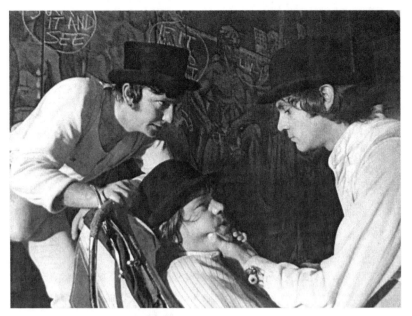

In this image from Stanley Kubrick's 1971 film A Clockwork Orange, *Alex and his "droog" Dim harass a man.* © AF archive/Alamy.

dren turned the Volkswagen "beetle" into the "love bug" and could not buy Japanese gadgets fast enough. When their parents made fun of the British, calling them "Limeys" and other derogatory names, their children welcomed the Beatles and the Rolling Stones with nose-thumbing enthusiasm and made "swinging" London the hip fashion capital of the world with Carnaby Street at the epicenter. In other words, the children of the World War II generation set about systematically dismantling the value structure in which their parents had—innocently, proudly, but relentlessly—imprisoned them.

Burgess Sees Society as the Villain

The story of *A Clockwork Orange* takes place sometime—in the near future when teenage rebelliousness has provoked police-state response. The teenagers speak a street slang laced with graphic neologisms [newly coined words] and bastardized Russian called "Nadsat." Street gangs mug and rape at will, and kids drink narcotic-laced milk. The story is narrated by fifteen-year-old Alex, who, along with his three mates, is given to mugging lonely pedestrians, robbing tobacconists' shops, and the like. Alex explains how his buddies ("droogs") got him arrested for beating up ("tolchocking") an old woman ("starry ptitsa") whose death gets him imprisoned. To get out, he volunteers for the "Ludovico treatment," which conditions him to avoid his three main joys: sex, classical music, and "ultra-violent" behavior. The treatment consists of watching the most appalling torture films while under the influence of an emetic drug. One film, a documentary about Nazi atrocities, is accompanied by the music of [Ludwig van] Beethoven, whose Ninth Symphony is Alex's favorite.

This aversion therapy cures Alex of his violent impulses— and of his love for great music. On his release from prison he becomes the pawn of a protest movement dedicated to the abolition of forcible conditioning for violent criminals. Some readers find the Burgess dilemma too equivocal: Which is worse, the disease or the cure? Burgess blames society for both, and cult followers tend to prefer to draw this conclusion, insisting that society creates the conditions in which criminal behavior flourishes and then, in an attempt to cure the problem, devises methods of conditioning that dehumanize those whose behavior is labeled criminal. . . .

Burgess . . . has it both ways. While he deplores brainwashing and blames society for Alex's problems, he is reluctant to endorse human nature in the raw. It is a position that many cult readers find attractive, a "pox on both houses," a curiously passive attitude that makes them feel morally superior at no spiritual expense.

Burgess blames the excesses of human nature on a repressive society that corrupts its citizens—and primarily its youth—by restricting their liberty and force-feeding them outmoded values. Thus, their natural rebellion gets out of hand and only leads to more repression. It is a vicious cycle, and at the end of *A Clockwork Orange*, Burgess seems to wash his hands of the whole thing. In fact, he later labeled the book "too didactic, too linguistically exhibitionistic," thus justifying the complaint of some critics that he both raised and rendered moot the question of good and evil. What he is doing is nothing more than following in the footsteps of cult authors like [German writer Johann Wolfgang von] Goethe and [19th-century British writer] Walter Pater, and even J.D. Salinger, who, after publishing works that inspired cult followings, later had second thoughts about what they had done.

A Clockwork Orange Becomes a Cult Favorite

The fact that both the film and the book shocked older readers was all it took to make *A Clockwork Orange* attractive to young people. What they saw that their elders tended to miss was the spirit of black comedy that informs the work. Alex and his "droogs" are a parody of street gangs, and the crimes they commit, whether they are exaggerated or accidental, are stylized in a way that is more theatrical than threatening. Indeed, many of the scenes have a choreographed look, like an intergalactic road-show version of *West Side Story*.

Cult readers (and viewers) also enjoyed the mockery of classical music. Having been brainwashed to believe that all great music is uplifting, they delight in watching Alex do unspeakable things while under the influence of Beethoven's Ninth [Symphony], with its hymn to joy vibrating through the Dolby speakers as Alex mugs and maims. Later, when the same music is used to accompany films of Nazi atrocities, and to condition Alex to vomit at the sound, cult enthusiasts were delighted to see classical music thus desanctified.

Thus, cult followers in general ignored both [Stanley] Kubrick and Burgess in turning this work into a cult favorite. They were too busy enjoying the rebellion to worry about its cause or to want to change things. They were enjoying a liberation that their sheer numbers and an affluent society were making possible to a degree never before imagined. They were having too much fun fighting their own little fantasy war against the hopelessly square refugees from the swing era. Alex reminded them of Mick Jagger, one of the heroes of this war, a war that counted among its casualties such idols as Jim Morrison, Jimi Hendrix, and Janis Joplin.

It is interesting to note that the movie version of *A Clockwork Orange* had to be edited down to an R-rating after receiving an X-rating that excluded the only audience young enough to be interested in it. There is classic irony operating here, because both the book and the movie are serious, adult fare; yet the audience for both was the same audience that would later turn *The Rocky Horror Picture Show* into the top cult movie classic of all time. This serves as a reminder that cult books (and films) are defined by their readers and audiences, not their authors and producers.

Burgess's work has been dismissed as a minor dystopia, an allegation more in keeping with the spirit of cult followers than that of the general reader who might fear the consequences of a permissive society that has gotten completely out of hand. Rather than blaming Burgess's grim forecast on a society that is too repressive, the general reader is more likely to believe that society has not been repressive enough. Cult followers of the early seventies, however, had little interest in concepts like utopia or dystopia, for they had no historical perspective with which to judge such things. They would have agreed with Henry Ford when he said, "History is bunk." As far as they were concerned, the past was ancient history—and bad example. Depressions? Wars? Why couldn't older people get their act together?

What cult followers saw in *A Clockwork Orange* was an electronically charged age in which teenagers ruled the roost and quadraphonic sound systems could reach hitherto unheard of decibel levels. Of course they also saw the inevitable assault of the storm troopers in the form of parents and other leaders of society who swoop down on fun-loving teens and drag them off to concentration camps that hide under such euphemisms as rehabilitation centers, detox clinics, correctional facilities, and intervention programs.

Alex thus took on the status of a heavy-metal hero, psychologically lobotomized by an insensitive society. If his appearance and behavior flirt with fascism, it is something cultists are not likely to admit, even though this is not the first cult book to suggest such a leaning. Cultists are extremists, and extreme political positions are often indistinguishable. The fact that Burgess puts his "fascist" thugs in a "communist" setting and attracts a cult illustrates this point.

One popular myth that helps explain the appeal of *A Clockwork Orange* is the myth of the gangster as hero. The criminal as outcast was one of Fyodor Dostoevsky's favorite motifs, and ever since Romanticism glamorized the misfit, outlaws have seized the imagination. It is not the lawlessness of the gang that matters as much as the gang as outcast, as an outnumbered few pitted against the tyranny of the majority.

The classic western (book and movie) thrived on this myth, and its presence could be felt in the age of the gangster film. And, of course, it was glorified for all time in *West Side Story*. In more recent times, it has found its way into such youthful favorites as *The Outsiders* and *Colors*, not to mention dozens of forgettable sci-fi stories in which teams of vigilantes confront lawless hordes.

In *A Clockwork Orange* there is the presence of yet another myth, one that can be found only between the lines. This is the myth of the Pied Piper. Burgess was in his mid-forties when he wrote this book. Whatever his avowed purpose, he succeeded in becoming a modern-day Pied Piper who led great numbers of children down a very strange path. But he must share the dubious honor of leading the willing young down the primrose path of protest with that sly old trickster Kurt Vonnegut Jr.

[George] Orwell's *1984* still chills the blood of readers young and old, and [Aldous] Huxley's *Brave New World* leaves most readers feeling decidedly uncomfortable, but the reaction then, and to some extent now, to *A Clockwork Orange* can be summed up in the comment made by one young man, a college freshman who had read the book and just seen the movie: "Groovy!" Nobody has ever said that about the Orwell or Huxley books.

A *Clockwork Orange* Depicts a Society Beyond Redemption

Robert O. Evans

Robert O. Evans is emeritus professor of English and comparative literature at the University of New Mexico. He is the author or editor of numerous books of literary criticism, including William Golding: Some Critical Considerations.

The violence in A Clockwork Orange *is caused by man's fallen nature in combination with his faulty political systems, according to Evans in the following viewpoint. The book is not political in nature, Evans claims, for Burgess sees little difference between Russia and the United States. Burgess holds both nations responsible for the spread of a violent youth subculture to England.*

[*A* Clockwork Orange and *The Wanting Seed*] are heavily larded with violence, so much so that, were they not set in the future, and identifiable with a number of other works with similar concerns, such as [Yevgeny] Zamyatin's *We* or [George] Orwell's *1984*, one might suspect Burgess of borrowing a page from the French *nouveau roman* [new novel] and hanging his two 1962 books on fictive structures dependent on violence for their very shapes. To quote Neville Chamberlain, and disagree with him, we have not found much "peace in our time." . . .

Man's Fallen Nature Is Responsible for Violence

[Of] what does *A Clockwork Orange* warn us? Social conditions over which we have no control? It is rather . . . an expression of disgust and revulsion about what has happened to society in our lifetimes. It does not warn us to be careful not to follow a certain political course, as do most of the other books in the [dystopian] convention. It is, to be sure, a subtle work, often pointing a finger at what Burgess considers to be the cause of our situation. The climate of violence, of which Alex is the teenaged exemplar, exists in a Britain in the near future, and the possibility exists that it is man's fallen nature, in conjunction with his institutions, that has brought about this dreadful situation. The book does not deal with the consequences of political action. It is not an attack on a Soviet-like system, though one can hardly doubt that the author had little use for a Russia that could send [Andrei] Sinyavsky and [Yuli] Daniel to a concentration camp, and [Andrei] Sakharov to exile and psychological rehabilitation, for speaking the truth as they saw it. Neither is it an attack on the permissive society of the United States, though Burgess implies that at least part of the fault in the England he depicts can be blamed on the two giant superpowers. The violence of the young gangsters is generally considered to be an American trait; the language they speak has close relations to Russian, as I have also said. Burgess tells what he thinks about the superpowers: "As for America, that's just the same as Russia. You're no different. America and Russia would make a very nice marriage." . . .

Neither *A Clockwork Orange* nor *The Wanting Seed* really fits the dystopian convention Burgess inherited. He borrows some of its devices, but at heart his statements are different. In these novels it is the statement about mankind, not the fictive structure in which it is embedded, that matters. If we search a little deeper, we may conclude that Burgess in these books is really closer to Jonathan Swift than Orwell or Zamyatin. We may discover, if we push matters a bit, that he is really closer to [John] Milton's *Paradise Lost* than any of his predecessors in the dystopian convention. What Zamyatin is saying is that if we persist on the Soviet political course we may destroy something in our society and in ourselves which is precious (though a racial memory may remain). Burgess is saying that because of what we are (translate because of man's fallen nature) something dreadful is bound (or at least likely) to happen and happen quite soon—we can already see the beginnings (especially in *A Clockwork Orange*). . . .

[Burgess] is even more so an experimental novelist, more than Zamyatin, more than [Alain] Robbe-Grillet and the other writers in the school of the *nouveau roman*, more (perhaps because he is so indefatigable) than any other writer in English today. He has sought since his very early book *A Vision of Battlements* (in which, he says, he simply set out to recall his wartime experiences in Gibraltar) to find new ways of expressing devastating truths, not perhaps so subtly as the French novelists but quite as deliberately. His force is language while theirs perhaps is structure. This is the light, then, in which I think his dystopian works should be read. We may fault him on several grounds, primarily for not having always written well-made books, but not for any ambiguity of intention. His dystopian works are not calculated as warnings but rather as expressions of what he considers to be the truth of the human condition.

Burgess Has a Pessimistic View of Human Nature

Bernard Bergonzi

Bernard Bergonzi is a British educator, literary critic, novelist, and poet. He is professor emeritus of English at the University of Warwick and the author of numerous works on British writers.

A striking feature of A Clockwork Orange *is the way in which Burgess writes about horrible violence with humor, comments Bergonzi in the following viewpoint. Alex is shown to be remorselessly evil and likeable—suggesting that people are drawn to evil because they choose it, not because they are victims of society, Bergonzi argues. The critic concludes that Burgess has a pessimistic vision of human nature and a romantic view of evil.*

In *A Clockwork Orange* Burgess [explores] the kind of spiritual life that might, in fact, lead to damnation. This novel, which is, I think, Burgess's most brilliant and blackest achievement, is set in a shabby metropolis at some unspecified time in the future, where teenage gangs habitually terrorise the inhabitants. The story is told by one of them in the first person, in a superb piece of mimetic [exhibiting mimicry] writing. This narrator is morally but not mentally stunted; he writes an alert, witty narrative in a special kind of slang that incorporates a large number of words of Russian origin; one is never told the social or political events that underlie this linguistic intrusion, but it is possible that Burgess is trying to comment, in a mirror-image fashion, on the current dominance of Americanisms in colloquial English speech. The invention of this idiolect [language or speech pattern] is an ex-

Bernard Bergonzi, "Between Nostalgia and Nightmare," *The Situation of the Novel*, pp. 149–87. Pittsburgh: University of Pittsburgh Press, 1970. Copyright © 1971. Reprinted by permission of the University of Pittsburgh Press.

traordinary achievement; it is hard to read at first, but with a little persistence it can be mastered, . . . in fact, after a second reading of *A Clockwork Orange* I found myself starting to think in it. One of its functions is to keep at a certain distance the horrors that Alex, the young narrator, so cheerfully describes: to say, 'we gave this devotchka a tolchok on the litso and the krovvy came out of her rot' is less startlingly direct than, 'we gave this girl a blow on the face and the blood came out of her mouth'.

Alex Is Cheerfully Amoral

Alex is cheerful, even high-spirited in his life of crime: Older citizens, particularly of a square or bourgeois disposition, are fit material for beating up; books are to be destroyed, and girls are to be assessed by the size of their breasts, and raped where possible. In *A Clockwork Orange* none of this behaviour is ascribed, as contemporary psychologists or sociologists would have it, to a mindless protest against lack of love or cultural deprivation or the alienating structures of capitalist society. Alex makes it clear that he has chosen evil as a deliberate act of spiritual freedom in a world of sub-human conformists. Despite everything—and this is, perhaps, the most disturbing thing about Burgess's novel—Alex is engaging. His adventures are often funny, or at least his way of describing them is: Whereas [Kingsley] Amis and [Angus] Wilson keep comedy and horror on separate planes in their fiction, Burgess, like [Evelyn] Waugh, often fuses them. In some respects Alex is not at all a stereotype delinquent. He and his friends, having robbed and beaten an elderly couple in a shop, make off with the takings and then buy innumerable drinks and presents for a couple of old women in a pub, partly to secure an alibi for themselves, but also out of pure generosity. Alex spurns pop songs and is a passionate listener to classical music, which inspires him to thoughts of violence and rape, sometimes to the point of orgasm.

Alex does not, in short, reflect an exact sociological understanding of present-day youth and its problems. Burgess uses him to illustrate his own quasi-theological conviction that men do extreme evil because they choose to, and enjoy doing it, rather than because they are reluctantly or unconsciously forced to it by social conditioning. In presenting Alex, Burgess has drawn on a familiar literary tradition. [Herbert] Marcuse has spoken of the way in which bourgeois society

> remained an order which was overshadowed, broken, refuted by another dimension which was irreconcilably antagonistic to the order of business, indicting it and denying it. And in the literature, this other dimension is represented *not* by the religious, spiritual, moral heroes (who often sustain the established order) but rather by such disruptive characters as the artist, the prostitute, the adulteress, the great criminal and outcast, the warrior, the rebel-poet, the devil, the fool—those who don't earn a living, at least not in an orderly and normal way.

In the language of [Charles] Baudelaire or [T.S.] Eliot this is the opposition between the masses of the spiritually dead and null, and those who, however evil they may be, are at least alive. [Honoré de] Balzac's Vautrin stands some way behind Alex, but his more immediate literary antecedent is Pinkie in Graham Greene's *Brighton Rock*, the articulate, lucid, cruel, young Catholic diabolist. Alex is more alive, and less improbable than Pinkie; yet he remains the embodiment of a literary idea, a late instance in the milieu of the cosh and the bicycle chain and the gang bang, of the romantic antinomian [denying the obligation to adhere to moral law] cultivation of evil.

There Is No Virtue in Coerced Goodness

Eventually Alex is caught by the police, and after being roughed up by them and imprisoned, he is selected for a new form of remedial treatment, since the prisons are now all needed for political offenders, and common criminals are to be rehabilitated and permanently 'cured'. Alex is given an intensive course of aversion therapy; he is injected with a drug and shown films of brutality and sexual assault, accompanied by classical music. Eventually he is cured of his taste for all three, since any hint of them causes uncontrollable nausea. (The music is regarded by the authorities not as having any aesthetic or spiritual dimension, but merely as something that arouses unwelcome emotional excitement in Alex.) After the course Alex is released, a good citizen, yet a person in whom the capacity to choose has been wholly destroyed. In his account of the therapy Alex undergoes, Burgess is describing known techniques, and it is here that the novel acquires philosophical profundity: In what sense is a man who has been *forced* to be good better than a man who deliberately asserts his humanity by choosing evil? For the behaviouristic pragmatism that invents such procedures, the question is presumably meaningless; but genuine humanists will recognise its urgency, even if they cannot fully answer it. Towards the end of the novel Alex gets caught up in a political plot against the government and is exploited by the opposition (very much as Ralph Ellison's Invisible Man is used by the Communists); in a final unexpected twist of circumstances, the government reverses Alex's treatment, and he ends the novel as a free individual with all his criminal impulses—and his love of music—restored. Many of Burgess's assumptions are, of course, vulnerable. The notion of 'spiritual death' is a powerful literary idea, but it is existentially specious; it is merely a way of reinforcing one's sense of the otherness of other people. Non-Augustinian [referring to the teachings of St. Augustine, a philosopher who believed that because of original sin, man is a fallen creature] Christians as well as conventional progressives will want to object to the extremity of Burgess's pessimism, as well as his basically romantic conception of evil. Nevertheless, as an embodied imaginative vision of life *A Clockwork Orange* is hard both to forget and to refute, and in its emphasis on the nature of human freedom in a totalitarian society the book has philosophical as well as literary importance. As a novel of ideas that projects a conservative and pessimistic view of human nature, *A Clockwork Orange* seems to me to have a similar quality and significance to William Golding's *Lord of the Flies*, while being more humorous and less diagrammatic. One wishes that it had achieved the same reputation.

Burgess Has a Hopeful View of Human Nature

Geoffrey Aggeler

A professor, literary critic, novelist, and short story writer, Geoffrey Aggeler is professor emeritus of English at the University of Utah and a visiting professor in the writing program and drama department at the University of California at Santa Barbara.

In writing A Clockwork Orange, *Anthony Burgess was reacting against sociologists of the time who were promoting the use of conditioning prisoners and violent youth gang members to be good, Aggeler relates. In the final chapter of the novel, an older Alex finds a life of violence less appealing than settling down and raising a family. This chapter demonstrates Burgess's belief that a fallen man can learn from his mistakes and repent, Aggeler maintains.*

Although [*A Clockwork Orange*] can be read as an answer to and a rejection of the main ideas of B.F. Skinner, the author of such works as *Walden Two* and *Beyond Freedom and Dignity*, Burgess seems to have been directly influenced less by Skinner's ideas in particular than by accounts he had read of behaviorist methods of reforming criminals that were being tried in American prisons with the avowed purpose of limiting the subjects' freedom of choice to what society called "goodness." This struck Burgess as "most sinful," and his novel is, among other things, an attempt to clarify the issues involved in the use of such methods.

Burgess Was Influenced by Russia

The setting of *A Clockwork Orange* is a city somewhere in either western Europe or North America where a civilization has evolved out of a fusion of the dominant cultures east and west of the Iron Curtain. This cultural merger seems to be partly the result of successful cooperative efforts in the conquest of space, efforts that have promoted a preoccupation with outer space and a concomitant indifference to exclusively terrestrial affairs such as the maintenance of law and order in the cities. As it does in *The Wanting Seed*, Pelagian [a belief system that denies original sin] faith in *A Clockwork Orange* also accompanies Promethean fire [relating to Prometheus, a Greek mythological figure who stole fire from heaven]. Appropriately, there is shop looting on Gagarin Street, an avenue of this Western metropolis, and a victim of teenaged hoodlums is moved to ask, "What sort of a world is it at all? Men on the moon and men spinning around the earth like it might be midges round a lamp, and there's not no attention paid to earthly law nor order no more."

In light of recent events [in 1979], a reader is apt to assume Burgess was thinking of the United States when he envisioned this situation of the future. In fact, he was more directly influenced by what he had seen during his visit to Leningrad in 1961. At that time, Russia was leading in the space race, and the gangs of young thugs called "stilyagi" were becoming a serious nuisance in Russian cities. At the same time, London police were having their troubles with the young toughs known as the "teddy boys." Having seen both the stilyagi and the teddy boys in action, Burgess was moved by a renewed sense of the oneness of humanity, and the murderous teenaged hooligans who are the main characters in *A Clockwork Orange* are composite creations. Alex, the fifteen-year-old narrator/protagonist, could be either an Alexander or an Alexei. The names of his three comrades in mischief, Dim, Pete, and Georgie, are similarly ambiguous, suggesting both Russian and English given names.

A reader may miss these and other hints completely but what he cannot overlook is the effect of culture fusion on the teenage underworld patois [nonstandard language] in which the story is narrated. The language itself, Burgess's invention, is called *nadsat*, which is simply a transliteration of a Russian suffix equivalent to the English suffix *teen*, as in "fifteen." Most, although by no means all, the words comprising nadsat are Russian, and Burgess has altered some of them in ways that one might reasonably expect them to be altered in the mouths of English-speaking teenagers.

Implements of street warfare, such as bicycle chains, knives, and straight razors, bear their unaltered Russian names, which seem much more suggestive of the objects themselves than their English equivalent. A bicycle chain, for instance, its shiny coils shaken out along a sidewalk or whizzing through the night air, is so much more like an "oozy" than a "chain." There is something much more murderous about a "cutthroat britva" than a "cutthroat razor." . . .

Burgess Was Appalled by Behavioral Conditioning

The novel is much more than a linguistic tour de force. It is also one of the most devastating pieces of multipronged social satire in recent fiction, and, like *The Wanting Seed*, it passes the test of "relevance." Although most people have been made aware of the assumptions of behavioral psychology through the recent uproar caused by Skinner's polemical restatement of his ideas in *Beyond Freedom and Dignity*, it is perhaps less generally realized that Skinner's schemes for imposing goodness on the human "mechanism" are among the less radical of those being proposed by behavioral technologists. As of this writing, a sociologist, Professor Gerald Smith of the University of Utah, is engaged in promoting the development of a device that can be implanted within the person of a paroled convict. The device, which measures adrenalin, is designed to send signals to a receiver in the home or office of his parole officer if the convict becomes excited by committing a crime. How this gadget would separate criminal stimuli from activities such as lovemaking that might signal "false positives" has not been revealed. What is certain, at least in the mind of the sociologist, is that the beneficial effects of such devices would completely justify their use. A convict would lose nothing, since, as a prisoner, he is already without freedom, and the benefits to society would be incalculable.

It is this line of thinking that Burgess challenges in *A Clockwork Orange*. He had been reading accounts of conditioning in American prisons, and it happened that as the teddy boys were being replaced on the streets by the mods and rockers, and youth was continuing to express its disdain for the modern state, a British politician put forward very seriously a proposal that obstreperous British youth should be conditioned to be good. At this point, Burgess says, "I began to see red and felt that I had to write the book." His protagonist Alex is one of the most appallingly vicious creations in recent fiction. Although his name was chosen because it suggested his composite Russian/English identity, it is ambiguous in other ways as well. The fusion of the negative prefix *a* with the word *lex* suggests simultaneously an absence of law and a lack of words. The idea of lawlessness is readily apparent in what we see of Alex's behavior, but the idea of wordlessness is subtler and harder to grasp, for Alex seems to have a great many words at his command, whether he happens to be snarling at his droogs in nadsat or respectfully addressing his elders in Russianless English. He is articulate but "wordless" in that he apprehends life directly, without the mediation of words. Unlike the characters who seek to control him and the rest of society, he makes no attempt to explain or justify his actions in terms of abstract ideals or goals such as "liberty" or "stability." Nor does he attempt to define any sort of role for himself within a large social process. Instead, he simply experiences life directly, sensuously, and, while he is free, joyously. Indeed, his guiltless joy in violence of every kind, from the simple destruction or theft of objects to practically every form of sexual and nonsexual assault, is such that the incongruous term *innocent* is liable to come to a reader's mind.

Alex also has a fine ear for European classical music, especially [Ludwig van] Beethoven and [Wolfgang Amadeus] Mozart, and although such widely differing tastes within one savage youngster might seem incongruous, they are in fact complementary. Knowing his own passions, Alex is highly amused by the idea that great music is any sort of "civilizing" influence. . . .

At First, Alex Freely Chooses Violent Crime

The first third of the novel is taken up with Alex's joyful satiation of all his appetites, and as rape and murder follow assault, robbery, and vandalism, we are overwhelmed by the spectacle of pleasure in violence. Although it might be argued that such psychopathic delight could not be experienced by a sane person, there is no implication in the novel that Alex is anything but sane—sane and free to choose what delights him. Since his choices are invariably destructive or harmful, it appears that society's right to deprive him of his freedom, if not his life, could hardly be disputed. What the novel does dispute is society's right to make Alex something less than a human being by depriving him of the very ability to choose a harmful course of action. . . .

When Alex is finally caught (while attempting to escape from a burglary involving a fatal assault on an old woman) it is mainly because his gang has betrayed him and facilitated the capture. He is sentenced to fourteen years in prison, and it is here that he will feel the effects of a major change in government policy. . . .

Alex, who brings attention to himself by murdering a fellow inmate, is selected as a "trail-blazer" to be "transformed out of all recognition."

Alex Is Stripped of Choice

The purpose of Alex's transformation is to eliminate his capacity to choose socially deleterious courses of action. Psychological engineers force upon him what Professor Skinner might call "the inclination to behave." Strapped in a chair, he is forced to watch films of incredible brutality, some of them contrived and others actual documentaries of Japanese and Nazi atrocities during World War II. In the past, violence has given him only the most pleasurable sensations; now he is suddenly overcome by the most unbearable nausea and headaches. After suffering a number of these agonizing sessions, he finds that the nausea has been induced not by the films but by injections given beforehand. Thus his body is being taught to associate the sight or even the thought of violence with unpleasant sensations. His responses and, as it were, his moral progress are measured by electronic devices wired to his body. Quite by accident, it happens that his body is conditioned to associate not only violence but his beloved classical music with nausea. The last movement of Beethoven's Fifth Symphony accompanies a documentary on the Nazis and the connection of the two with bodily misery is thus firmly fixed.

Finally, when his rehabilitation is complete, he is exhibited in all his "goodness" before an audience of government and prison officials. What is demonstrated on this occasion beyond all argument is that his body will not permit his mind to entertain even the thought of violence. When a hired actor insults and beats him, Alex must force himself to respond in a truly "Christian" manner, not only doing but willing good for evil. In a desperate effort to ease his misery, he literally licks the man's boots. . . .

A further demonstration proves that Alex is above sexual violence as well. When a ravishing, thinly clad young morsel approaches him on the stage, he is filled momentarily with an old yearning "to have her right down there on the floor with the old in-out real savage," but again his visceral "conscience" prevents him and he is able to stop the nausea only by assuming an almost Dantesque attitude of non-carnal adoration. Having thus gratified his rehabilitation engineers with proof that he is a "true Christian," Alex is free to enter society again—if not as a useful citizen, at least as a harmless one, and as living proof that the government is doing something to remedy social ills and thus merits reelection.

Alex is not only harmless but helpless as well, and shortly after his release he is the victim of a ludicrous, vengeful beating by one of his most helpless former victims, an old man assisted by some of his ancient cronies. Unable to endure even the violent feeling needed to fight his way clear, he is rescued by three policemen. The fact that one of his rescuers is a former member of his own gang and another a former leader of a rival gang suggests that the society is experiencing a transitional "Interphase" as it progresses into its Augustinian phase [referring to St. Augustine's philosophy that because of original sin, man is a fallen creature]. These young thugs, like the "greyboys" in *The Wanting Seed*, have been recruited into the police force apparently on the theory that their criminal desires can be expressed usefully in the maintenance of order on the streets....

Not surprisingly, Alex's former associates find his new situation ideal for settling some old scores. They drive him down a lonely country road and administer more than "a malenky bit of summary" with their fists. Then, in a battered and even more helpless condition, he is left to drag himself through pouring rain toward a little isolated cottage with the name HOME on its gate. This little cottage happens to have been the scene of one of the most savage atrocities he and his droogs had carried out before his imprisonment, and one of the victims, a writer named F. Alexander, is still living in it. F. Alexander had been beaten up by Alex and his gang and forced to watch the four of them rape his wife, who had died as a result. The writer has remained in the cottage devoting all his energies to combatting the evils of "the modern age." Right-fully blaming government failure as much as teenage savagery for his wife's death, he seeks to discredit the government suffi-ciently to have it turned out of office in the next election. . . .

Alex Becomes a Victim

Since Alex and his droogs had been masked during their as-sault on HOME, F. Alexander does not recognize him. Filled with indignation against the state, he sees only another "vic-tim of the modern age" who is in need of compassion. It soon occurs to him, however, that Alex can be used effectively as a propaganda device to embarrass the government—an example of the dehumanizing effects of its crime-control methods. He calls in three associates who share his beliefs and his enthusi-asm for this idea. Although F. Alexander and his friends seem motivated by the loftiest of liberal ideas, it soon becomes ap-parent that they are incapable of seeing Alex as anything but a propaganda device. Like [Jonathan] Swift's "projectors," they are so full of the abstract and the visionary that they have little concern for the suffering or welfare of individual human beings. To them Alex is not an unfortunate human being to be assisted but "A martyr to the cause of Liberty" who can serve "the Future and our Cause." . . .

In his anger, Alex lapses from polite, respectful English into snarling nadsat, a slip that, along with a few others, causes F. Alexander to remember the night his home was invaded. Al-though he cannot be certain that Alex was one of the attack-ers, his suspicions begin to grow, and it is apparently because of this that a change is made in the plan for using Alex. The revolutionaries had originally planned to exhibit Alex at pub-lic meetings to inflame the people, but now they decide to make him a real martyr to their cause. Lest the people not be sufficiently shocked by the destruction of Alex's moral nature, they decide to have him destroyed completely by the govern-ment. As a dead "witness," he will be even more damning than a "living" one. They lock him in a flat and fill it with sounds of a loud and violent symphony in the hope he will be driven to suicide. Since he had already been considering suicide, the plan is immediately successful and he dives out a window, severely although not fatally injuring himself. . . .

[While] Alex is recovering in a hospital from his death dive, a power struggle rages. The government receives ample amounts of embarrassing publicity concerning the attempted suicide, but somehow survives. One day Alex awakens to find himself fully as vicious as before his treatment. More psychological engineers, using "deep hypnopaedia or some such slovo," have restored his moral nature, his "self," and his concomitant appetites for Beethoven and throat cutting. As he listens to the "glorious Ninth of Ludwig Van," he exults,

> Oh, it was gorgeosity and yumyumyum. When it came to the Scherzo I could viddy myself very clear running and running on like very mysterious nogas, carving the whole litso of the creeching world with my cut-throat britva. And there was the slow and the lovely last singing movement still to come. I was cured all right.

The Augustinians are delighted. In this "depraved" condition, he cannot embarrass them further.

Burgess Believes in the Possibility of Redemption

At this point, the American edition of *A Clockwork Orange* ends, and Stanley Kubrick, following the American edition very closely, ends his film. In its earlier British editions, however, the novel has one additional chapter that makes a considerable difference in how one may interpret the book. This chapter, like the chapters that begin the novel's three main parts, opens with the question, "What's it going to be then, eh?" Indeed, this is the question the reader has been left to ponder. We have seen Alex's depraved "self" replaced by a well-behaved "not-self," which is then replaced by the old "self" when he is "cured." We are led to believe that, aside from imprisonment or hanging, these two conditions are the only possible alternatives for Alex. The omitted chapter, however, reveals yet another alternative. Alex and a new squad of droogs are sitting in his old hangout, the Korova Milkbar, drinking hallucinogenic "milk-plus mesto" and getting ready for the evening. This is exactly the way the novel began, but whereas the opening chapter is a prelude to violence, this one reveals Alex becoming weary of violence. He leaves his gang and wanders alone through the streets reflecting on the changes in his outlook. Although the behavioral engineers have managed to restore his old vicious self, he is becoming sentimental and starting to yearn for something besides the pleasure of indulging himself in classical music and the "old ultra-violence." What it is, he does not know, but when he encounters a member of his old gang who has married and settled down to a completely harmless, law-abiding existence, he realizes that this is what he wants for himself. He wants to marry and have a son. He will try to teach his son what he knows of the world, but he doubts that his son will be able to profit from his mistakes. . . .

[If Burgess] has an Augustinian view of man as a fallen creature, he also has a great deal of non-Augustinian hope for him as a creature of growth and potential goodness. The message of the chapter that was omitted is that, if there is hope, it is in the capacity of individuals to grow and learn by suffering and error. Suffering, fallen human beings, not behavioral technology or the revolutionary schemes of idealists, bring "goodness" into the world. Awaiting this development is of course far less efficient or satisfying to some than imposing a design that ensures "goodness," but there is reason to hope that the wait will be worthwhile. Burgess is far more optimistic than Skinner, who has obviously lost all faith in man as he is and as he may become without the imposition of goodness.

Alex Displays Hostility Toward Women in *A Clockwork Orange*

Deanna Madden

Deanna Madden is a professor of English at Hawaii Tokai International College.

The violence in A Clockwork Orange *is troubling because Anthony Burgess appears to be condoning rape and violence against women as preferable to the loss of free will through behavior modification, Madden contends. Furthermore, Burgess links rape with eroticism and admits he found vicarious pleasure in writing about rape and violence against women. It is inescapable to conclude that Burgess himself is hostile to women and believes them to be inferior to men, the critic argues.*

The future society of *A Clockwork Orange* is a violent world in which the weak are at the mercy of the strong. Like [Aldous Huxley's] *Brave New World* and [George Orwell's] *1984, A Clockwork Orange* portrays a patriarchal culture in which women are subordinated and peripheral. Women are perceived through the male gaze, in this case that of a fifteen-year-old delinquent, Alex. While Alex's views may reflect his immaturity, they are also a reflection of the culture in which he lives. In the Russianized teenage slang, or "nadsat," there are many words for females: "devotchka" (girl), "sharp," "cheena," "ptitsa" (a vulgar-sounding word which seems to stress their bodies . . .), "baboochka," "lighter," and "forella" (the last three used only for old women). To Alex females are sexual objects perceived mainly in terms of their "groodies" (breasts). The three girls at the milk bar in the first chapter are typical teenaged females of their society: The silver badges they wear announcing the names of boys they have slept with before age fourteen suggest their promiscuity. It is a society in which females are initiated into sexuality at a tender age and often violently: The two girls whom Alex picks up at the "disc bootick" and then rapes are only ten years old, as is the girl menaced by Billyboy and his droogs.

Women Are Alex's Victims

Alex regards females primarily as objects to rape. His attitude toward women is one aspect of his violent rebellion against society. Destructive and antisocial, he is a criminal who robs, assaults, and rapes, a sociopath who takes pleasure in venting his aggression and inflicting pain. Women are vulnerable to the violence Alex represents because he is stronger and they weaker. He demonstrates these violent sexual politics when he and his droogs rob a convenience store by assaulting the owner's wife and ripping her clothes. Later the same evening, still seeking thrills, they break into a house and brutally gang-rape another woman as the culmination of their night of violence.

Old women, doubly vulnerable because of age and gender, are also victims in the novel. Alex's mother is a passive woman who tries not to aggravate her dangerous son. He perceives her as one of the "pitiable" old. She is powerless to influence him: to make him attend school, to keep him from his street violence, or even to persuade him to turn down the volume of his loud music. The old women at the Duke of New York pub are also intimidated by Alex. They are easily bullied and bribed by Alex's gang to provide the young delinquents with alibis during their crime sprees. An old woman who lives alone with a houseful of cats is Alex's last female victim. Although he is

In this image from Stanley Kubrick's 1971 film A Clockwork Orange, *Alex talks to two teenage girls. To Alex, females are sexual objects perceived mainly in terms of their physical appearance.* © Sunset Boulevard/Corbis.

apprehended by the police during this break-in, he manages first to kill the old woman with a fatal blow.

Choosing Violence Is Better than Having No Choice

Alex's violence toward women (and the elderly) in the early chapters of the novel make him a sort of monster from whom the reader tends to recoil. However, when Alex becomes in turn the victim of the police, who brutally beat him, and of Dr. Brodsky and Dr. Branom, who make him the guinea pig in their diabolic experiment with the Ludovico technique (behavior modification designed to turn him into a model citizen), Alex becomes a more sympathetic character. Forced to watch horrifying films of rape, assaults, and war crimes, he is made nauseous with injections until he comes to associate violence with nausea. Alex begins to seem like a naif compared to the corrupt state which has him at its mercy. Burgess suggests that, compared to the state's crimes, Alex's crimes are small. Burgess is more alarmed by the power of the state to eradicate the individual's free choice and turn him into a machine. By using the Ludovico technique, the state plays God and interferes with the most important aspect of man—his free will. Worse yet, if the state can control Alex with this behavior modification technique, it can control others and by this means become all-powerful.

Thus, Burgess wishes the reader to view the violence which Alex and his droogs have committed as a form of choice. The reader is expected to perform the mental gymnastics of seeing that, viewed from a certain angle, violence is good, that Alex the rapist is preferable to Alex the clockwork orange. When the conditioning is reversed and Alex is returned to his old violent self, it is a victory for free will.

While this message is difficult for many readers to accept since it appears to condone violence and in particular violence against women, another disturbing aspect of the novel is its tendency to equate rape and eroticism. Throughout most of the novel Alex's first and only impulse toward women is to rape them. He appears unable to relate to them in any other way or to feel sexually attracted without the urge to be violent. The result is to offer only two extremes of male sexual behavior. This becomes clear in Alex's appearance before a live audience after he has successfully undergone the Ludovico technique. When a nubile young woman is presented to him, he must suppress his urge to rape her to avoid the nausea it triggers. Instead he responds to her platonically, as if he is the knight and she the damsel on the pedestal. The ridiculousness of this response is made clear by the titters of laughter it elicits from the audience. Dr. Brodsky also suggests there is an obvious connection between violence and eroticism: "The sweetest and most heavenly of activities partake in some measure of violence—the act of love, for instance; music, for instance." Curing Alex's aggression amounts to emasculation. After his cure, he cannot defend himself, enjoy [Ludwig van] Beethoven (the violent classical music he prefers), or experience erotic desire. Released from prison, he is a mere shell, anxious to lose himself in drugs, depressed, and suicidal.

Women Are Still Objects to a Reformed Alex

When *A Clockwork Orange* was first published in the United States in 1963, it omitted a final chapter that had appeared in the British edition. The difference in endings makes a considerable difference in the impression left with the reader by the novel, as Burgess notes in his introduction to the revised American edition (1988), which includes the missing chapter. The first ending leaves the impression that Burgess endorses the violence of the clockwork orange society, for Alex's return to his old violent self is a victory for the individual. He has won out against the state which would control him. Burgess explains that he wanted instead to show that his "young thuggish protagonist grows up. He grows bored with violence and recognizes that human energy is better expended on creation than destruction. Senseless violence is a prerogative of youth. . . ."

In the restored final chapter Alex, now age eighteen, feels vaguely dissatisfied with his life. The teenaged girls at the milk bar no longer attract him. In his wallet he carries a picture of a baby clipped from a newspaper. When he encounters his old droog Pete, now married to a pretty young woman, he is envious and begins to fantasize, in Burgess's words, "a different kind of future." In his fantasy he imagines "coming home from work to a good hot plate of dinner" prepared by a "ptitsa all welcoming and greeting like loving." But in his vision this "ptitsa" is vague, a faceless female whose main attributes are her ability to cook a hot meal, to have a fire burning on the hearth, and to welcome him home with open arms. She is less important than the child she will bear him—the baby in the next room. In true patriarchal fashion, Alex envisions the baby as a boy. The idea that he might father a daughter apparently never occurs to him. At this point in his reverie he forgets the woman, as if once she has borne his son, she is no longer important, and contemplates at length his relationship with his imaginary future son. But obviously there will be no son until first there is a mate, so he tells himself that what he must do next is find "some devotchka or other who would be a mother to this son." She is, it seems, just a necessary next step in achieving his ultimate goal—an heir. Thus, while the final chapter shows Alex turning away from rape and violence, his image of women merely changes from targets of rape to useful breeders. He never sees them as human beings equal to himself.

Burgess's Own Attitude Toward Women Suggests Misogyny

It might be argued that Alex's attitude toward women reflects his own warped mentality and the violence of his clockwork orange culture, not Burgess's views, but the salient feature of violence remains, especially violence against women. Then there is the disturbing linking of eroticism and rape. Alex's final attitude toward women as breeders of sons also calls into consideration Burgess's own attitudes toward women, since this is where he ultimately wishes to lead the reader. The focus is not only on a male protagonist who has failed to figure out any way of relating to females except to rape them, beat them, impregnate them, or, as in the case of his mother and his future wife, to be served by them, but on a male who ultimately only relates to another male, his mirror image, his son.

Critics have suggested that the misogyny to be found in Burgess's work may have its roots in his personal life. His mother died when he was two years old, his stepmother did not love him, and his first wife, to whom he was married for twenty-six years, was repeatedly unfaithful to him [according to biographer John J. Stinson]. In his autobiography *Little Wilson and Big God*, Burgess describes this marriage as marked by many infidelities on both sides. The curiously neutral manner in which he relates his wife's infidelities conceals how he felt about them, but the reader infers he must have been hurt by her refusal from the beginning of their relationship to be exclusive. Burgess implies that since she chose to be unfaithful, he saw no reason why he too should not be. In spite of the adulteries, he claims to have loved her. The issue of female promiscuity arises in *A Clockwork Orange* in the form of the devotchkas in the milk bar with their silver medals and the ten-year-old girls who wear padded bras and lipstick.

Another influence on Burgess's attitude toward women was no doubt his Roman Catholicism. While Burgess now considers himself a lapsed Catholic, his work is permeated by ideas drawn from the Catholic Church, such as the doctrine of original sin. Burgess is a highly moral writer, interested in man's spiritual dimension and his relation to God (or "Bog" in *A Clockwork Orange*). According to his autobiography, the early influence of Catholicism caused him to regard sex as sinful and instilled in him feelings of guilt.

Burgess Displays a Callous Attitude Toward Rape

One of the most brutal scenes involving a female in *A Clockwork Orange* is the gang rape of F. Alexander's wife. Burgess has confessed that this incident had its origins in an assault on his wife in 1944 by four men [according to biographer Samuel Coale]. While the assault was brutal (Burgess's wife Lynne was kicked unconscious and subsequently suffered a miscarriage), it was not a rape. Burgess, who was stationed in Gibraltar at the time, felt anger at the American GI deserters who had attacked her and at his commanding officers for refusing him leave to rush to her. Both in his wife's promiscuity and in her assault, Burgess must have felt a lack of control over her body. By rewriting the incident as a rape which the husband is forced to watch helplessly, he includes his own feelings of anger, frustration, and guilt.

Elsewhere Burgess's comments on the subject of rape, however, must strike a female reader as remarkably callous. He admits in his introduction to *A Clockwork Orange* that in writing the novel he "enjoyed raping and ripping by proxy." These are not emotions that the typical female reader would share. When he dismisses Alex's acts of violence, including rape, as a sort of phase that Alex will outgrow, the female reader may balk. Does Burgess really expect us to agree that "senseless violence is a prerogative of youth"? Is it simply a part of growing up that young males should rape? And when Alex observes that his son will probably do all the things he has done, should we feel no shiver of horror?

Kate Millett in *Sexual Politics* points out that the threat of rape in a patriarchal society can be an "instrument of intimidation." It is a way of keeping women subordinate. She also notes that "patriarchal societies typically link feelings of cruelty with sexuality, the latter often equated with evil and power." Perhaps this helps to explain why rape is linked to eroticism in Burgess's novel. But clearly rape is an act of aggression in which the chief motive is to inflict hurt and thereby assert the rapist's power. As Millett explains, "In rape, the emotions of aggression, hatred, contempt, and the desire to break or violate personality take a form consummately appropriate to sexual politics."

The world of *A Clockwork Orange* is a distorted mirror world of London in the early 1960s and also of Russia. Many of its images are identifiable reflections of a contemporary society which regards young women as sex objects and exploits them. In the convenience store which Alex and his droogs rob stands "a big cut-out showing a sharp [female] with all her zoobies [teeth] going flash at the customers and her groodies [breasts] near hanging out to advertise some new brand of cancers [cigarettes]." The novel also reflects contemporary society's devaluation of the older woman, who having lost her youth and attractiveness, finds herself powerless and despised.

The dystopian visions presented in [*Brave New World, 1984*, and *A Clockwork Orange*] present bleak prospects for women. All three reflect the times from which they emerged and their authors' reactions to those times. None of the authors conceived of a future that would place males and females on an equal footing. . . . But more disturbing than the obvious inequality in these novels are the hints of outright hostility toward women, such as the intimation that they are intellectually and morally inferior to men, that they are physically disgusting, and that there is nothing terribly wrong in raping them. Perhaps the most frightening aspect for women is how prevalent these attitudes are among male authors, as this sampling of possibly the three most important twentieth-century dystopian novels shows. So far as one can tell, Huxley, Orwell, and Burgess did not intend to express misogyny. They were simply putting down on paper their artistic visions.

Burgess Uses Violence to Underscore the Irrationality of Existence

John J. Stinson

John J. Stinson is professor emeritus at the State University of New York College at Fredonia.

Anthony Burgess creates a world of violence perpetrated by Alex and his mates that is both brutal and engaging, writes Stinson in the following viewpoint. Using vivid descriptions, humor, and an imagined language, the writer succeeds in making Alex an appealing character and distances the reader from the horror of his violent actions. Although many critics argue that the evidence in the novel suggests otherwise, Burgess insists that Alex chooses violence of his own free will, the critic notes. He goes on to say that Burgess believes that it is preferable to choose evil and violence than to have no choice.

Alex, killer, rapist, sadist, and maker of general mayhem at age fifteen, is, in fact, one of the mouthpieces for Burgess's own ideas. Addressing the reader about people's shocked dismay when confronted with manifestations of evil, he expresses a rather amazingly sophisticated anti-Pelagian [referring to the denial of original sin and the importance of free choice] view:

> this biting of their toe-nails over what is the *cause* of badness is what turns me into a fine laughing malchick. They don't go into what is the cause of *goodness*, so why of the other shop? If lewdies are good that's because they like it, and I wouldn't ever interfere with their pleasures, and so of the other shop. And I was patronizing the other shop. More,

John J. Stinson, "Dystopias and Cacotopias," *Anthony Burgess Revisited*, pp. 47–63. Boston: Twayne, 1991. From John J. Stinson, EBK: ANTHONY BURGESS REVISITED, 1E. Copyright © 1991 Cengage Learning.

badness is of the self, the one, the you or me on our oddy knockies and that self is made by old Bog or God and is his great pride and radosty. But the not-self cannot have the bad, meaning they of the government and the judges and the schools cannot allow the bad because they cannot allow the self. And is not out modern history my brothers, the story of brave malensky selves fighting these big machines? I am serious with you, brothers, over this. But what I do I do because I like to do.

Burgess Insists Alex Exercises Free Choice

Burgess insists that Alex's actions, atrocious assaults and all, proceed from deliberate choices of his own free will. The question, "What's it going to be then, eh?," which opens all three parts of the novel, and the last chapter as well, reinforces the idea that people are free to choose their own actions. Some readers have felt that Burgess has to shout this point at them because it goes against the evidence. Alex is, in their view, something very much like a robot programmed for violence, or, if not quite that, a young man who acts out in disturbed fashion a universal need to assert life and independence in a tyrannously dull society. Their point is that whether he likes it or not, Alex's life has been heavily molded by his environment. If the environment were not so oppressively constrictive, Alex would not have the need to act out his rebellion so outrageously. Thus, environment has made Alex what he is, and it is the job of the behavioral psychologist to prescribe the means whereby emotional imbalances may be redressed. In insisting that Alex acts out of free choice, these readers maintain, Burgess has disregarded his own evidence. These are the readers, then, more inclined to accept the claims of Drs. Brodsky, Branom, and cohorts to the effect that they are not doing something that goes against nature by conditioning Alex toward the good; rather, they are removing the "error" of some past conditioning that inclined Alex so heavily toward "the old ultra-violence." Actually, the free will/

determinism conflict in the work of Burgess, as in that of most writers, takes the reader down a dark, tricky, winding road.

Burgess Denounces the Behaviorists

Thematically, the behaviorists in the novel are portrayed as not particularly intelligent villains. Burgess's anti-behaviorist stance in the novel is so pronounced that the print media have felt that Burgess cast himself as the bête noire [meaning a person strongly detested] of B.F. Skinner, thus virtually announcing himself as available on call to refute any proclamations of the renowned behaviorist about necessary abridgments of freedom and dignity. Burgess very unfairly stacks the deck against the behaviorists, say many who regard *A Clockwork Orange* as a thesis or philosophical novel. In the novel the behaviorists are pliant tools of a totalitarian state. They employ Ludovico's technique on Alex because the authorities need to get his type out of the prisons to accommodate hordes of political prisoners (the Interphase obviously having begun, liberal belief in basic goodness has apparently given way to sore disappointment because of the likes of Alex). The behavioral psychologists are seen as two-dimensional, uncultured shrinkers of the soul, clumsy in the application of procedures they themselves have devised. Dr. Brodsky says of music, "I know nothing about it myself. It's a useful emotional heightener, that's all I know." He is unconcerned that the radical aversive conditioning process—Ludovico's technique—has destroyed Alex's enjoyment of [Ludwig van] Beethoven along with his ability to carry out violence.

Burgess's short novel inclines toward the fable, and it is unreasonable to expect that its socio-philosophical ideas are argued with the concentrated weight and scrupulous fairness with which they would be argued in an academic treatise. Burgess's novel did, though, so memorably strike some decidedly contemporary chords that it provided a ready reference point for certain social issues that were seriously, and heatedly, debated in the real world. By the mid-1970s aversive conditioning was making headway in the U.S. penal system: Some inmates were given shots of apomorphine, inducing violent vomiting and dry retching; others were given Anectine, which produces agonizing sensations of suffocation and drowning; sex offenders were given electric shocks to the groin. Such practices were generally successfully opposed by the American Civil Liberties Union and other groups as "cruel and unusual punishment"; *A Clockwork Orange* was almost always at least mentioned in media reports about litigation connected with this troubling but ethically complex issue.

Burgess Employs Imaginative Violence

A Clockwork Orange stayed in the news because of the currency and vigor of its ideas, but it is a significant work of literature for other reasons. Burgess employs black humor and the grotesque—two highly favored forms of the late sixties— more integrally, and therefore more successfully, than any other writer of the period with the possible exceptions of Joseph Heller and Günter Grass. What might be referred to as the "violent grotesque" is employed at the very outset as the demonically engaging Alex recounts for us, his "brothers," with relish and a delicious savoring of detail, how he and his "droogies" (gang mates) perpetrated various nightly horrors: an old man returning from the library is insulted and assaulted; his false teeth are ripped from his mouth and crunched by the stomps of the teens' heavy boots; heavy-ringed knuckles slam into the old man's bared gums until his mouth is a riot of red; he is stripped and kicked for good measure. This is only the very beginning of violence that exceeds that of [the Marquis] de Sade in intensity if not imaginativeness. Storekeepers, husband and wife, are brutally beaten and robbed; a writer's wife (Mrs. F. Alexander) is savagely gang-raped in her home and her husband is forced to watch

This image from Stanley Kubrick's film adaptation of A Clockwork Orange *shows Alex and his "droogs" assaulting an old man.* © Archives du 7eme Art/Photos 12/Alamy.

helplessly; two barely pubescent girls of ten are raped; an old woman (the Cat Lady), a well-to-do recluse, meets her death trying to defend herself and her valuables during a robbery. All this—and more—is accomplished by Alex, Dim, Pete, and George on the two consecutive days that comprise part 1, eighty-four pages of the novel.

Burgess Distances the Reader from Violence

The high level of Burgess's black comic craft is testified to by his ability to make us approach the vicious assault of an old lady with something very much like mirth and excitement. Burgess writes in his introduction to the new American edition that his "intention in writing the work was to titillate the nastier propensities of my readers." He might be thought almost to prove his theological (Augustinian) point by the success with which he carries out his intention. Readers come to have ambivalent feelings only when their moral reactions, linguistically stupefied into unwatchfulness, suddenly rouse themselves and come panting up indignantly. By the near miracle of his craft, particularly by his linguistic inventiveness,

Burgess has succeeded in temporarily making his readers one with the wantonly brutal young assaulters:

> He [the old man returning from the library] looked a malenky bit poogly when he viddied the four of us . . . coming up so quiet and polite and smiling, but he said: "Yes? What is it?" in a very loud teacher-type goloss, as if he was trying to show us he wasn't poogly. . . . "You naughty old veck, you," I said, and then we began to filly about with him. Pete held his rookers and George sort of hooked his rot open for him and Dim yanked out his false zoobies, upper and lower. He threw these down on the pavement and then I treated them to the old boot-crush, though they were hard bastards like, being made of some new horrorshow plastic stuff. The old veck began to make sort of shumbling shooms—"wuf waf wof"—so Georgie let go of holding his goobers apart and just let him have one in the toothless rot with his ringy fist, and that made the old veck start moaning a lot then, then out comes the blood, my brothers, real beautiful. So all we did then was to pull his outer platties off, stripping him down to his vest and long underpants (very starry; Dim smecked his lead off near), and then Pete kicks him lovely in his pot, and we let him go.

What forestalls reader revulsion at this basically realistic scene of violence is distancing through the use of invented language. "It is as if we were trying to read about violence in a foreign language and finding its near-incomprehensibility getting in the way of a clear image," Burgess says in a *New York Times* piece. The distinct teenage language serves also to re-awaken the reader's awareness of the anarchic impulse of the teenager and the instinct to be one with the herd, to regard other groups just as "other," utterly alien, in no way like the self. . . .

Alex Is Portrayed Sympathetically

The most important function of the language is the softening of the otherwise unbearably repulsive violence, but the violence itself is thematically integral. Not at all pornographic, the grotesque violence is the means by which Burgess attacks the failures of rationalism. While it has proved difficult to define the grotesque precisely, many commentators seem to agree that it frequently involves the sudden subversion of the apparent world of order and form by the shocking appearance of the absurd, purely irrational, or primally chaotic. Naïve liberals and rationalists willfully shut their eyes to primal discords, but they are forced open by the "horrorshows" staged by [an Adolf] Hitler or an Alex. Frequently used as a means of exposing the naïveté of excessive rationalism, the grotesque is associated with [Joseph] Conrad's Kurtz [character in *Heart of Darkness*], the liberal humanist who, in quick descent, comes to preside over "unspeakable rites"; and [William] Golding's Piggy [character in *Lord of the Flies*], the bespectacled emissary of rationalism whose precious brain is spilled grotesquely out on a rock. Alex is a producer of the grotesque, but Alex is in all of us, which is the point that Burgess most cleverly gets across as he disorients his readers just enough by the language to cause them vicariously to share the thrill of cruelty.

Alex (his name seemingly suggesting "without law") is more an extraordinary teenage rebel than he is Satan or even Dionysus [God of wine and fertility] (as Burgess's own ending makes clear), but he has a winsome effect on the reader because, in a world of pale neutrals, he has energy and commitment. (By contrast, Alex's parents "rabbit" every day at mindless jobs, stare vacuously each evening at insipid programs on the telly, and retire to bed, sleeping pills in their bloodstreams, lest they be awakened by the blast of Alex's stereo.) From the beginning we sympathize with Alex because he is, in his own words, "our faithful narrator" and "brother." This is an old novelistic trick, readers tending to sympathize with anyone, save a total monster, who continually tells them about his life and makes them vicariously share it. Then, too, Alex has wit, some intelligence, a love of classical music, his gift of pungent language, and a kind of artistry in his violence. We react with sympathy and pathos when Alex falls into the clutches of the state, particularly when it attempts "rehabilitation" by reducing him to a "clockwork orange." This term is explained by F. Alexander, Burgess's mock double and another ironic mouthpiece, a pompous sort who has just completed a flatulently styled tome titled *A Clockwork Orange*: "The attempt to impose upon man, a creature of growth and capable of sweetness, to ooze juicily at the last round the bearded lips of God, to attempt to impose, I say, laws and conditions appropriate to a mechanical creation, against this I raise my sword-pen."

Alex does become a clockwork orange temporarily when, in order to gain a much speedier release from prison, he assents to Ludovico's technique. The "therapy" consists of showing Alex atrocity films after he has been given a drug to induce pain and nausea. The association of violence and nausea incapacitates Alex from further violent action, any attempt instantaneously provoking literal wretchedness. Released, Alex finds himself quickly at the mercy of all those whom he had previously victimized. In a schematic plot framework . . . designed to show retributive justice in action, each of these victims pays back the now defenseless Alex. One of those who gets the satisfaction of a payback is F. Alexander, reputedly—and, in his own mind—an idealist and bastion of liberal values. His view of man had gone untested, however. An unsuspected part of himself powerfully leaps out when he discovers that Alex was one of the rapists responsible for his wife's death. Very much human, he is not above the philosophy of an eye for an eye. This is one of Burgess's "proofs" that evil is endemic in man, that it has always been there and always will be. Another proof is found in Alex's prison reading: the "big book," the Bible, in which he "read of these starry yahoodies tolchocking each other and then peeting their Hebrew vino and getting on to the bed with their wives' like handmaidens, real horrorshow."

Even Violence Is Preferable to Conditioning

Alex suffers greatly—emotionally, mentally, and even physically—as a result of the Ludovico "therapy." Burgess's point is
clear, since, in fact, it is presented somewhat didactically
through a third spokesman in the novel, the prison charlie;
but Burgess's expression of it outside the novel is even clearer:
"What my and [Stanley] Kubrick's parable tries to state is that
it is preferable to have a world of violence undertaken in full
awareness—violence chosen as an act of will—than a world
conditioned to be good or harmless." Not to be able to choose
is not to be human. If evil were somehow to be eradicated, its
opposite—goodness—would, having no meaning, cease to exist. "Life is sustained by the grinding opposition of moral en-
tities," Burgess writes in the introduction to the new American
edition. In most discussions that the book has generated this
prime thematic point has generally been agreed with. The ex-
postulations of B.F. Skinner have, though, given some listeners
serious pause. Basically (most notably in *Beyond Freedom and
Dignity*), Skinner argues that the very survival of the race de-
pends upon the surrender of some freedom, as that term has
been historically understood. No Augustinian [referring to St.
Augustine, who believed that because of original sin, men existed in a fallen state and needed God's grace to be saved],
Skinner also pleads that we examine carefully the operant
conditioning that underlies people's choices to behave poorly.
He has made clear that his strong preference is always for
positive reinforcement rather than aversive techniques to correct maladaptive behavior. Burgess likes to make the point
that evil exists, and must exist, as a part of the human self; he
is fond of pointing out that "live" is "evil" spelled backwards.

Two Different Endings Offer
Opposing Messages

The novel's ending has always been problematic. Burgess's last
chapter, the twenty-first, was deleted from the first American
edition and all subsequent American editions until 1987. . . .

The twentieth chapter (chapter 6 of part 3) ends as the government authorities, under strong pressure from politically aroused public opinion, reverse the effects of the aversive therapy by deep "hypnopaedia," restoring Alex to his old self—he "viddies" himself "carving the whole litso of the creching world with my cut-throat britva." Chapter 21—the famous deleted chapter—presents a mellowing, increasingly reflective, eighteen-year-old Alex who is coming to see that his previous violent behavior was childishly perverse. He thinks of marriage, stability, and the son he one day hopes to have. He contemplates explaining to his son all his own past crimes as an admonition, but then thinks that he "would not really be able to stop him [prevent his son from enacting similar crimes]. And nor would he be able to stop his own son."

The truncated ending, which leaves the reader with a stark presentation of unregenerate evil, surely carries more impact. Burgess's own ending, besides having just a whiff of sentimentality about it, is easily exposed to ridicule. Detractors might say that it reduces the novel to a spectacular but largely meaningless comment on those oh-so-difficult teenagers and their problems of adjustment. Burgess prefers his own ending, with his own worldview, his own "theology." The truncated version, closing with a view of unregenerate human evil, would be a more fitting conclusion for a William Golding novel. With his own ending, Burgess implies a more nearly equal tug from the Pelagian and Augustinian poles, proving once again that he is not quite an Augustinian, and that he is a believer in eternally recurrent cycles. He writes that the Norton editors believed in 1962 that the last chapter "was bland" and "showed a Pelagian unwillingness to accept that a human being could be a model of unregenerable evil." The truncated ("Augustinian") version, he says was "sensational," but not a "fair picture of human life." No matter what the reader's perspective, *A Clockwork Orange* provides a picture that remains painted on the walls of the mind near the place where the conscious and subconscious meet.

Burgess Explores the Relationship Between Language and Violence in *A Clockwork Orange*

M. Keith Booker

M. Keith Booker is a professor of English at the University of Arkansas. He is the author of several books on science fiction, popular culture, and modern British and American literature.

In the following viewpoint, Booker points out the importance of language in A Clockwork Orange. *The language used by Alex and his friends differs from that of those in authority, distancing them from society and making it easier for them to justify their violent behavior. Although it may seem as if the musical nature of the language lessens the impact of the violence on the reader, on reflection this is not the case, Booker concludes.*

Language—especially the *control* of language—is often an important topic in dystopian fiction. One of the most striking uses of language in dystopian fiction occurs in [Anthony] Burgess's *A Clockwork Orange*, a dystopian fiction set in a nightmarish near-future England that centrally focuses on the "nadsat" dialect spoken by Alex, its narrator and central character. Alex is a teenage gang member, and this private dialect provides a private language in which he and his fellow delinquents ("nadsats") can communicate. Dr. Branom, one of the psychologists who participate in the later conditioning of Alex to remove his violent antisocial inclinations, explains the composition of nadsat language: "Odd bits of old rhyming slang. A bit of gipsy talk, too. But most of the roots are Slav.

M. Keith Booker, "Anthony Burgess: *A Clockwork Orange* (1962)," *Dystopian Literature: A Theory and Research Guide*, pp. 94–99. Westport, CT: Greenwood, 1994. Copyright © 1994 by ABC-CLIO. All rights reserved. Reproduced by permission.

Propaganda. Subliminal penetration." Indeed, most of the roots of nadsat words (including "nadsat," the suffix of Russian numbers from eleven to nineteen) do appear to be Russian, though the nadsats have anglicized some of them in colorful ways, as when *khorosho* ("good" or "well") becomes "horrorshow."

A Parody of Western Fear of Communism

There is, of course, a not-very-subtle irony in Branom's suggestion that the Russians have brainwashed the rebellious youth of Burgess's English dystopia, especially since brainwashing is precisely the job of Branom himself. One potential message of Burgess's book (echoing [George Orwell's] *1984* as it does in other ways as well) is thus that there is no point to turning England into a totalitarian state from within in order to resist the threat of totalitarianism from without. Indeed, this Russian invasion of the language of the teenagers of England would seem to function largely as a parody of Western paranoia over the potential influence of Communist infiltration on the hearts and minds of capitalist youths, though it is a sort of unstable parody that leaves open the possibility of an entirely straightforward interpretation. [Robert O.] Evans suggests that the use of Russian in *A Clockwork Orange* is mostly intended to enhance the dystopian atmosphere, as British and American readers will automatically associate Russia with oppression. Perhaps the nadsats really *have* been brainwashed by the Russians, a reading which suggests that Alex's conflict with British authority is not a confrontation between free choice and conditioning so much as a clash between two different conditioning programs. Indeed, though Alex himself at one point rejects the suggestion that his social environment may have contributed to his delinquency, it is rather naive to view Alex as entirely free before undergoing treatment by the Ludovico technique that makes him incapable of violence. Even if Alex and his fellow gang members have not been subtly influenced by Russian propaganda they, like everyone, have been exposed to a number of forming influences throughout their lives. In the book's final chapter (omitted from American editions of the book prior to 1987) Alex himself seems to recognize this point, comparing his early self to a wind-up toy. On the other hand, in *1985* Burgess seems to suggest that before his conditioning Alex does evil by his own free choice. Burgess further makes clear his support for the right to such a choice, arguing that "if I cannot choose to do evil neither can I choose to do good. It is better to have our streets infested with murderous young hoodlums than to deny individual freedom of choice."

An Imaginative Language Symbolizes Superiority

The nadsat language spoken by Alex and his mates at first appears to be a form of linguistic rebellion, a way of rejecting the official ideology of the society around them by rejecting the language of that society and replacing it with one strongly informed by the language of a feared enemy. For one thing, the plural sources of this language invest it with a heteroglossia [diversity of types of speech within a language] that powerfully opposes any attempt at the imposition of monological ideas. For another, this private language furthers a sense of solidarity among the nadsats that contributes to their resistance to the rule of official authority. In addition, the existence of this nadsat language gives the nadsats an inherent linguistic advantage over the representatives of authority; these official representatives cannot understand the nadsat language, but Alex understands conventional English quite well and can use it when necessary. When his "Post-Corrective Adviser" visits him to investigate his absence from school, Alex explains that absence in a language the adviser can understand: "'A rather intolerable pain in the head, brother, sir,' I said in my gentleman's goloss. 'I think it should clear by this afternoon.'"

Alex's adviser is not impressed, as it turns out, but this ability to speak a "gentleman's goloss" in addition to the nadsat dialect does give Alex a certain advantage. [Critic Theo] D'haen, who sees in Burgess's work a consistent belief in the positive power of language, thus suggests that the nadsat language shows the imaginative superiority of Alex and his fellows, while the inability to understand nadsat shows the lack of imagination and flexibility of the adults they encounter. . . .

A Language Replete with Violence

But, despite the fact that Burgess's delinquents seem to rape and pillage almost at will (at least after dark) in his dystopian London, superior power in *A Clockwork Orange* is still on the side of traditional authority, as Alex's fate indicates. Language may be a powerful determining factor in one's understanding of reality, and Orwell's Party may be able to manipulate reality by manipulating language, but that is largely because the Party has the *power* to enforce its version of reality in a way that Alex and the nadsats cannot. One cannot make official reality go away simply by modifying one's own language; one must also have the power to influence others to use that language, and this is a power that Alex and his friends lack. The nadsat language contributes to the alienation of Burgess's delinquents from the mainstream of British society, increasing the distance between them and ordinary citizens and thereby making it easier for them to justify the crimes of violence they commit against those citizens. But this language also invests the nadsats themselves with an air of otherness to mainstream society that makes it easier for the authorities to justify their own sometimes brutal reactions to the "ultra-violence" of the nadsats. Using their own language may increase the marginality of the nadsats to the society in which they live, but it does not make them entirely independent of that society.

In addition, while having their own language may combat the interpellation of the nadsats within the accepted English

of official society, the nadsat language has a powerful interpel-
lating effect of its own. The language is invested with a lust
for violence and a contempt for women, presumably because
the nadsats themselves harbor such attitudes. But one could
also argue that the nadsats harbor such attitudes largely because violence toward innocent citizens and contempt for
women are built into the language they use. Granted, there is
an almost poetic quality to the nadsat language, and the colorful expressions and musical rhythms of this language are
probably the most interesting features of Burgess's book. As
Michael Gorra notes, there is an aspect of pure literary experi-
mentation in Burgess's use of the nadsat language to narrate
his book, though it is certainly also important to keep in
mind that this language is not devoid of ideological content
but in fact implies a very specific attitude toward society and
the world. Gorra goes on to note that the use of this language
also endows Alex with a vivid individuality that reinforces his
role as a solitary self in conflict with the demands of a domi-
neering state. . . . The distinctiveness of Alex's language does
make him more vivid as a character, and he is such an unpleasant character that some such device is obviously necessary in order to prevent him from being merely loathsome,
thereby undermining his role as protagonist and representa-
tive of the right to free moral choice. At the same time, language is by its very nature social. Alex's language is not really
unique to him; it is the language of an entire group and it is
derived from the languages of other groups.

Language Distances the Reader
from Violence

A Clockwork Orange is unusual among dystopian fictions in
that the book itself is narrated in the language of a marginal
group rather than in that of official authority. But, just as dystopian fictions tend inherently to undermine the authoritarian
pretensions of the official languages represented in them, so

too is the nadsat language called into question within the framework of Burgess's book. This language is inescapably associated with the beatings, rapes, and murders that it is used to describe, and the almost musical quality of the language (echoing Alex's own love of classical music) thinly disguises the ideology of hatred and violence of which the language is the verbal medium. The unusual nature of the language of Burgess's text to a certain extent distances the reader from the horrors being narrated, thereby making them initially less repugnant, perhaps even luring the reader into a certain complicity with Alex's actions. But upon reflection the radical disjunction between the musical sound of Alex's language and the actual content of his narration may make the seductions of nadsat language seem nearly as repugnant as the crimes Alex uses it to describe and perhaps every bit as repugnant as the mind-manipulation of Orwell's Newspeak [in *1984*].

In the end, it is not language, but religion that Burgess seems to offer as an alternative to tyranny in *A Clockwork Orange*. In what can be read at least partially as a response to [B.F.] Skinner's *Walden Two*, Alex undergoes a program of conditioning that leaves him incapable of committing a crime, though it also robs him of much of his humanity. This conditioning has sinister implications, though Burgess acknowledges (like Skinner) that brainwashing and pacification of the type undergone by Alex are themselves a part of the Christian tradition; when Alex finishes his conditioning, one of the doctors in charge proclaims, "He will be your true Christian, ready to turn the other cheek, ready to be crucified rather than crucify, sick to the heart at the thought even of killing a fly." But on balance Burgess's book seems to support the traditional Christian notion that humanity should be granted free will, even if that will includes the choice to sin against God, or (in Alex's case) to commit violent criminal acts. Burgess himself has described the worldview of his dystopian fictions as "Hebreo-Helleno-Christian-humanist." He then compares his position to that of John the Savage in [Aldous Huxley's] *Brave New World*, citing the suggestion by Huxley's [Mustapha] Mond that John desires the right to be unhappy. But John's position is highly problematic and does not necessarily represent a favorable alternative to that of Mond himself.

Social Issues in Literature

CHAPTER 3

Contemporary Perspectives on Violence

Gangs Are Responsible for a Large Share of Violent Urban Crime

Melissa Klein

Melissa Klein is a journalist.

Belonging to a gang makes a teen more apt to engage in criminal activity, reports Klein in the following viewpoint. Although many teens may join gangs out of a desire for a sense of belonging or the belief that a gang will protect them, the reality is that gang members are more likely to be victims of violence than their peers, Klein states.

Members of the Bloods gang engaging in turf battles with rival gang the Crips—that might sound like something out of a movie, but it was real life for Seattle teen Jon Amosa. The Bloods, founded in Los Angeles, are one of the biggest gangs in the country. It considers the Crips, another L.A.-based gang, its enemy. Amosa, 18, joined a local chapter of the Bloods at the age of 14, enticed by cousins who were already members.

Amosa was "jumped in"—beaten by other gang members—as an initiation rite. Then he went on to beat up members of rival gangs. "Whatever my 'big homey,' or the older guy, whatever they told me to do, I'd go do it, no questions asked," says Amosa.

In addition to fighting, he sold and used drugs. While rap stars may brag about being a thug or "gangsta," Amosa, now 18, says it was anything but cool. "I've lost a lot of friends to

Melissa Klein, "Gang Grief: Violence Wounds Teens and Communities," *Current Health 2, a Weekly Reader Publication*, vol. 35, no. 7, March 2009, p. 26. Copyright © 2009 by The Weekly Reader Corporation. Reprinted by permission of Scholastic Inc.

gang violence, a lot of family members too," he says. "Really, it's not worth it." Amosa left the gang after becoming more involved in his church.

A Growing Threat

Gang violence claimed the lives of 6 teens in the Seattle area in an 8-month period last year [2008] and left many others injured. Such violence can affect whole communities, not just people involved in gangs. Recent incidents across the country include the following:

- A curfew for teens was imposed in Hartford, Conn., after a bloody weekend in which 11 people were shot, including a 7-year-old boy. The shootings are believed to be gang related.
- A Kansas City, Kan., teen was sentenced to life in prison for a shooting that killed a 2-year-old girl. The teen, a gang member, was ordered to fire at the house where the girl was staying with her grandparents, according to court testimony.
- A gang brawl in Nyack, N.Y., north of New York City, was sparked when a high school student ripped a bandana with rival gang colors off the neck of a fellow student.

The most serious gang activity is centered in larger cities, such as Los Angeles, New York, and Chicago. Gangs are also present in suburbs and small towns, says James C. Howell, senior research associate at the National Youth Gang Center.

The center's 2006 National Youth Gang Survey shows there are about 26,500 youth gangs in the United States, with 785,000 members total. Gang members are responsible for a large share of the violent crimes committed by teens in large urban areas, studies show. In Seattle, gang members were responsible for 85 percent of the robberies committed by teens in 1998.

One study found that 8 percent of 12- to 17-year-olds joined a gang at some point in their middle or high school years. And almost a quarter of students surveyed in 2005 said there were gangs in their schools, up from 17 percent in 1999, says Howell. Gangs aren't just a guy thing, either: Experts estimate that up to 33 percent of gang members are girls.

Chantelle S., a 15-year-old from New York City, says many students in her high school are gang members. Fights sometimes break out between rival groups, leading the school to impose lockdowns with increased security. "It's kind of scary because you never know what can happen," she says.

Thug Life

What exactly is a gang? It's not just a group of people getting together to hang out. "If there's no criminal activity, then you are not a gang. A social group is not a gang," says Arthur Lurigio, professor of psychology and criminal justice at Loyola University, Chicago. Some gang members are barely teenagers, while others are your parents' age. The level of involvement in the gang may also vary from hard-core members to wannabe gangsters, Lurigio says.

Gangs give teens increased avenues to become involved in criminal activity, says Lurigio. "If you are in a gang, you are more likely to be committing every type of crime. You are more likely to carry a weapon, you are more likely to drop out of school," he says.

What makes gangs attractive to teens is the promise of a sense of belonging that they might not have at home or at school. They also join to be around older cousins or family members. Amosa says he did not have a strong relationship with his parents growing up.

That experience is common. "The gang becomes the parent for many kids. It becomes the school, the church," says Carl Taylor, professor of sociology and senior fellow at Michigan State University in East Lansing. He says gangs appeal to kids who feel they don't fit in elsewhere because the gang "will embrace you, will give you a sense of belonging."

Teens also join gangs because of the mistaken belief that membership will protect them. But gang members are more likely to be victims of crimes than people not in gangs, Howell says. And the risks of gang membership extend to the entire community, with some neighborhoods terrorized by drug dealing or robberies. In New York City, a teen was killed standing at his bedroom window after a member of the Bloods allegedly fired a gun in the air.

Experts say that the glamorization of gang life in music videos, video games, and movies fuels the desire to belong to one or just dress and act like a "G" (or gangster). But gang life often turns out to be very different from what members imagined. Several studies have found that most people who join gangs drop out within a year because the experience is not what they thought it would be, Howell says. Short-term members typically can leave gangs without consequences, although sometimes they are "beaten out" by other members.

"It looks as if it's going to be an idyllic life of protection, fun, [and] excitement," Howell says. But looks can be deceiving, he adds. "It's a rough life."

On Second Thought

Eddie Flores knows how rough and violent gang life can be. The 23-year-old Los Angeles resident speaks to students about gangs through the violence-prevention program Youth Alive!

At 14, he began hanging out with a "party crew," a group of teens that can be a gateway to more formal gang membership. He sold drugs and stole cars. Flores eventually dropped out of school, was arrested, spent time in jail, and was later shot in two separate incidents.

The second shooting happened when Flores was 20 and part of a group that wasn't a formal gang. But gang members confronted him, insisting that he was from a rival gang and was invading their turf. The bullet left Flores paralyzed from the chest down.

When he talks to teens from his wheelchair, Flores doesn't sugarcoat what happened to him. Instead, Flores encourages them to make better choices. "If I would have stayed away from the people who were having fun and I was hanging around more with the people who were into studying and being in school," he says, "my life would have been very different right now."

Teens Take Action

Fed up with gang violence in their communities, teens from across the country are coming together to work on solutions. They met in regional groups for 5 months and then came together at World Vision's Youth Empowerment Summit in Washington, D.C., to bring suggestions to Congress.

Stephanie V., 17, of Cicero, Ill., says she got involved in the project because she wanted to take action. There is a lot of gang violence in the community where Stephanie goes to high school, and some of her friends date gang members. "I think it's a huge problem," she says.

The recommendations the group came up with included providing better after-school programs and more job options to keep teens out of trouble. Amosa thought meeting other teens at the summit was helpful. "To see other cities fighting for the same cause that we were, that inspired us to do even more work," he says.

Positive Alternatives Must Be Offered to Get Teens to Reject Gangs and Violence

William R. Brownfield

William R. Brownfield is the assistant secretary, Bureau of International Narcotics and Law Enforcement Affairs.

There are compelling reasons for undereducated, impoverished youth to join gangs, suggests Brownfield in the following viewpoint. Among these are peer pressure and a sense that they have few options to break out of a cycle of poverty. Both positive and negative incentives need to be offered to keep teens out of gangs, Brownfield maintains. The positive incentives include education, prevention, and training, he states.

Once upon a time, there were 7 countries located in a long isthmus between two large continents. And not long ago—let's say the 1970s—most of those 7 countries entered a time of tremendous violence and civil conflict. Historians will debate for decades the cause of and blame for the violence, but there is no debate that the 1970s and 80s generated tremendous pressure in Central America, particularly the northern trio of Guatemala, Honduras, and El Salvador, to flee to safety. Hundreds of thousands did so. Many came to the United States for safety and a better life for their families.

There Are Gangs in Every Major U.S. City

As is usually the case in large migrant movements, the overwhelming majority were fine people who worked hard, educated their children, supported their families, and became

William R. Brownfield, "Gangs, Youth, and Drugs—Breaking the Cycle of Violence and Crime," remarks at the Institute of the Americas, US Department of State, October 1, 2012.

leaders in their communities. Some did not. They did not integrate into the larger communities. They did not adapt to the new culture and system. They organized themselves into groups outside their traditional communities and exploited their own communities through organized criminal activity. By the 1980s, they had organized in Southern California into two large groupings—Calle 18 or 18th Street, and Mara Salvatrucha 13 [MS-13]. Today, the FBI [Federal Bureau of Investigation] estimates there are more than 7,000 18th Street members and 5,000 MS-13 members in the Los Angeles area alone. And you will find members in every major city in the United States.

Is this an unusual phenomenon in U.S. history? Not really. In the second half of the 19th century, major cities on the East Coast confronted organized crime tied to the Irish immigrant communities. By the turn of the century, New York complained of a Jewish mafia grown from Eastern European migrants. And by the 1920s, most large cities confronted some version of the Italian mafia. Nor are gangs today unique to the Central American communities. When I grew up in the 1970s, I was warned not to mess with the Hell's Angels or Chicago's Blackstone Rangers, and they still exist today. The mafia has certainly not disappeared. But give 18th Street and MS-13 credit—they have surged into the lead.

The story continues, and it gets worse. Here in the United States, we deport foreigners who commit violent crimes, after they serve their sentences. I do not apologize for this. The American people never agreed to absorb the criminal population of the rest of the world. We have enough of our own, thank you very much. But as we deported gang members back to the northern triangle of Central America in the 1990s and first decade of this century, and without meaning or even realizing it, we sent seasoned criminals back to weak, vulnerable societies. Central America emerged from its nightmare only in the 1990s. They emerged with determination not to return to

Tens of thousands of undereducated and poorly prepared youth band together in criminal organizations. Positive alternatives must be offered to keep teens off the streets and out of gangs. © IS543/Image Source/Alamy.

those dark days, but also with weakened legal, judicial, law enforcement, and corrections institutions. Into these vulnerable communities thousands of criminals seasoned by gang activities in the United States were inserted. Not surprisingly, they found the same security, status, and wealth in gang structures that had worked for them in the north. We estimate [there are] as many as 85,000 18th Street and MS-13 members today in Guatemala, El Salvador, and Honduras. They maintained their connections in the United States and throughout Central America. And the more entrepreneurial among them established connections with the more sophisticated drug trafficking cartels headquartered in that large country located between Central America and the United States—Mexico.

And that, ladies and gentlemen, brings me finally to my topic of today: "Youth, Gangs, and Drugs—Breaking the Cycle of Violence and Crime."

Youth Without Hope Are Attracted to Gangs

We know the problem. Tens of thousands of disaffected, undereducated, and poorly prepared youth, seeing little hope for a future in their traditional communities, band together in criminal organizations. They consume the product of the illicit drug industry. They facilitate the logistics and transportation for the trafficking industry in Central America and Mexico and, in the United States, they are a primary distributor and retailer of the finished product. We also know the outlines for the solution to the problem. Thousands of youth in the United States and Central America do not join gangs because of a genetic predisposition to be criminals. They join because they see the gang structure offering the best options for life at their age, facilitated by a substantial amount of peer pressure. History teaches that to break them out of the gang structure, they must be convinced of the negative consequences of remaining in the gang and positive benefits for staying out. The carrot and the stick.

I am the assistant secretary of state for narcotics and law enforcement, sometimes referred to as the drugs and thugs bureau. I am normally associated with the hard side, the security side of international drug abuse. So let me begin with the stick. In 2008, at the same time the U.S. government announced the U.S.-Mexico Merida Initiative, we also announced an initiative for Central America. In 2010, this initiative matured into the Central America Regional Security Initiative, or CARSI. CARSI was and is paired with Merida because we realized that we cannot address the security and law enforcement challenge along the U.S.-Mexico border without also addressing Central America. And we cannot address the security, crime, drugs, and violence crises in Central America without addressing youth and gangs.

Under FBI management, we support programs in Guatemala, El Salvador, and Honduras to address directly the criminal gangs. The program involves training and equipping police to perform anti-gang law enforcement. But we also share intelligence and data bases. Remember, 18th Street and MS-13 have a large presence in both Central America and the United States. Personnel move back and forth. They communicate and coordinate. A phone call from a prison in El Salvador can be linked to a hit ordered in Washington, DC, Los Angeles, or even San Diego. But every time they move, communicate, or coordinate, they are vulnerable. This, ladies and gentlemen, is law enforcement, pure and simple.

We also support policing at the community level, because a better policed community is less attractive to organized gangs. In each country of the northern triangle, we support a model precinct program. In the most vulnerable and violent urban communities, we provide equipment, vehicles, training, communications, and social and economic programs for the community. In places like Mixco in Guatemala City and Lourdes in El Salvador, we have seen crime rates drop dramatically. The model precinct program does not attack the gangs directly; it takes away the space where they can operate.

We work with the three governments of northern Central America to control arms flows. A criminal gang is bad; a criminal gang armed with automatic weapons is much worse. We realize that many weapons flow into Central America and

Mexico from the United States. We also realize that the American people have been wrestling with the application of the Second Amendment for more than two centuries. But we have laws on the licensing and export of firearms that we can enforce. And by providing training and systems that help law enforcement track and identify data, we help law enforcement control the flow of sophisticated weapons to violent gangs.

Law Enforcement Targets
Violence and Drugs

CARSI's two principal targets are violence and drugs. Gangs are tied to both. And while not all gangs are drug traffickers, and not all drug trafficking is done by gangs, they are connected. CARSI is very aggressive in attacking the flow of drugs through Central America. We have supported, trained, and equipped specialized antidrug units throughout the isthmus. We have provided antidrug aviation capability to Guatemala and hope to provide the same to Honduras. We are working intensely in the Caribbean and Pacific to shut down maritime trafficking routes. We have strengthened laws and cooperation to attack illicit finance and money laundering. We are helping countries seize criminal assets and use them against such organizations. We are building cases and taking down the leadership of Central American drug trafficking organizations. Criminal gangs in Central America looking to make money from drug trafficking are finding plenty of stick and not much carrot.

Finally, we are working the often overlooked elements of law enforcement—prosecution, courts, and corrections. Efficient police coupled with inefficient rule of law and corrections systems do not solve the gang problem; they merely recycle it. Under CARSI, we work with the judicial systems of most Central American countries to review and upgrade criminal codes to reflect the 21st-century realities of gangs and drugs. We cooperate in efforts to upgrade and improve detention facilities to meet international human rights standards, but also to ensure that prisons do not become extensions of gang headquarters. The International Law Enforcement Academy in San Salvador provides state-of-the-art instruction and training to police, prosecutors, and investigators on responding to criminal gangs and drug traffickers.

Positive Alternatives Must Be Offered to Gangs

But breaking the cycle of youth, drugs, gangs, and violence requires more than just the sanctions of aggressive anti-gang policing, better community policing, fewer firearms, effective counter-narcotics, and improved rule of law. Law enforcement sanctions are an essential element to breaking the cycle. But it is not the only element. There must be an alternative offered to the gang member, or he will not leave the gang.

Part of the solution is education, prevention, and training. Youth with a basic education and an employable skill are not likely to join gangs. They do not need to join. They have better options outside the gang. In the past two years, we have worked with police in Central America to train over 12,000 students through the Gang Resistance Education and Training, or G.R.E.A.T., program. We are on pace to double that number this year. USAID [United States Agency for International Development] is an essential part of our CARSI strategy, and wherever my bureau establishes a model precinct program, USAID establishes a community development program. I have visited them in Guatemala, El Salvador, and Honduras. After visiting the renovated police station, I visit the church, community center, or job training site where former or potential gang members are offered a better future. Local leadership is essential. Family participation is essential. Police support is essential. If the gang member does not see a job waiting at the end of the community program, he will return to the gang. Unemployment is the life blood of the organized criminal gang.

Another part of the gang solution is rehabilitation for those coming out of the gang structure. Before they can be educated or trained, they must learn how to function as productive humans again. For the drug users, and this includes most gang members, rehabilitation starts with a clinical, medical process to wean them off their drugs. For many, this process starts in prison. The prison, in fact, may be the first place where the community and society have access to the gang member, and the opportunity to engage with the youth outside the gang structure. Of course prison is not a resort hotel. But it must serve a larger function than simply exacting society's vengeance for crimes committed in the past; a rehabilitated gang member is less likely to commit the same crimes in the future.

Finally, a public information campaign has to be part of the carrot for the criminal gang member. Public information is not just a bunch of posters hanging from telephone poles. To be effective, gang members must participate in the effort. They know what appeals to the youth gangs; they know how to reach them. Their participation becomes part of their rehabilitation and reentry into society. One reformed and successful former gang member is worth hundreds of outsiders in reaching and connecting with gangs.

Ladies and gentlemen, I am, obviously, not nearly as old as Ambassador [Charles] Shapiro, but I have recently crossed the threshold into my 60s. I am now old enough to remember fondly many of the lessons that my parents tried, unsuccessfully, to teach me 40 years ago. Youth will resist and rebel. That is what youth is all about; that is how we learn and mature. But the youth of today are the leaders of tomorrow. And far too many of them are embedded in gangs in North and Central America. Our communities can isolate, bypass, and quarantine them. But if we do so, we are failing as a society. For a society that cannot provide for its youth is a society guaranteed to fail. There is a way to break the cycle of violence between youth, gangs, and drugs. It takes years, but it took years for our societies to get into this situation. It takes clear and effective law enforcement sanctions, because permitting criminal activity without consequences is an open invitation for more crime. It takes education, training, and employment, because a society that cannot provide a hopeful future for its youth is a failed society.

I am an optimist. I believe we are on the right track. I believe this conference, its discussions and lessons learned, will move us further in the right direction. I look forward to the day when 18th Street is once again a route to bypass the White House on your way to the Mall in Washington and MS-13 is the winning square on a giant bingo board.

London Aflame: What Happens When You Let Teenagers Run Your Country

Jonathan Foreman

Jonathan Foreman, a former columnist for the New York Post, *is a research fellow at the Civitas think tank in London.*

Members of the left-wing in Great Britain attributed the London youth riots in the summer of 2011 to unemployment and oppression, claims Foreman in the following viewpoint. He goes on to argue that these commentators ignore the reality that most men in their teens and early 20s have an innate predilection for violence. The situation in London was made worse by the hands-off policy of the police, Foreman contends.

Yesterday, August 8 [2011], I was watching live looting footage—some of it from districts near mine or where friends were hunkered down behind locked doors—with appalled fascination, when the 1992 Los Angeles riots came to mind. It was not because here in London we have had anything like the savage assault on Reginald Denny or the gun battles between cops and street gangs. It was the reports from shopping districts where stores were in flames and the police nowhere to be found. It reminded me of that first day or so of the L.A. riots, when LAPD chief Daryl Gates allegedly held his officers back and allowed South Central to burn, just to show propertied Angelenos how much they needed him and his men.

Given the cuts in police budgets planned by the [prime minister David] Cameron government (which has "ring-

Jonathan Foreman, "London Aflame: What Happens When You Let Teenagers Run Your Country," *National Review*, vol. 63, no. 16, August 29, 2011, p. 21. Copyright © 2011 by National Review. All rights reserved. Reproduced by permission.

fenced" or increased money for foreign aid, climate-change prevention, and Britain's grossly inefficient health service), anyone could be forgiven for wondering whether the Metropolitan Police's leadership was allowing neighborhoods to burn to make an economic point.

If that was the plan, it was a foolish idea. The Cameron administration is dominated by liberal young men from privileged backgrounds or the media-marketing elite. They would never live in the kind of neighborhoods that bore the brunt of the violence, and who are unlikely to empathize with the white-working-class and immigrant shopkeepers whose stores were trashed and burned. Law and order has not been a Coalition priority, as should have been obvious from Cameron's notorious "hug a hoodie" campaign before the election, in which he called for more understanding of the alienated youths who make urban life a misery for the old and the weak.

But in any case, it has since become clear that London's Metropolitan Police was doing its feeble best, considering its inadequate equipment, training, and public-order doctrine, not to mention its poor leadership by politically correct apparatchiks. It was unprepared to counter the planned looting, which had been organized using mobile phones and social networks—though this has happened before in London, as well as in foreign cities hosting G12 and G20 summits. Worse, it foolishly assumed that sending small numbers of riot police—or rather police in riot gear—would intimidate looters into giving up and going home.

Instead, in some places, gangs of 30 or more hooded teens sent the cops scurrying in retreat. In other areas, the police stood their ground and bravely took the bricks and rocks hurled in their direction, but did not—perhaps could not—stop or disperse the youths setting fire to stores and sometimes the homes above them. They seemed to be waiting for the rioters to exhaust themselves and go home—which took

British police officers arrest a man as rioters gathered in Croydon, South London, in 2011. Violence and looting spread across some of London's most impoverished neighborhoods, with youths setting fire to shops and vehicles. © AP Images/Sang Tan.

many hours and much destruction. It was only where there were police horses and dogs—and there were too few equine and canine units to be in every riot area at once—that looters were driven off or arrested in significant numbers.

As usual, the Metropolitan Police did not equip its officers with baton rounds or tear gas or water cannon or any of the non-lethal riot-control technologies in standard use around the world. This was because, as its leaders subsequently said, with the support of the home secretary, the use of such weapons would represent an unacceptable escalation. It would signal a loss of control—as if burning department stores did not. It was telling that there were injuries among the police but none among the rioters. "The way we police in Britain is not through use of water cannon," claimed Home Secretary Theresa May. "The way we police in Britain is through consent of communities."

You can make of her peculiar logic what you will, but the sentiment is shared by the entire law-enforcement establishment in Britain, if not the ordinary constable in the street. Watching the footage of rampaging youths taunting the London police, I remembered how, when I was living in New York's East Village during the L.A. riots, there were the beginnings of a copycat riot in the neighborhood. A couple of hundred kids, many of them the anarchist youths who had taken over Tompkins Square Park that summer, marched up St. Mark's Place to Second Avenue and started breaking windows. A line of police appeared on the avenue—ordinary street cops, but many wearing helmets—and walked calmly but determinedly in the direction of the bottle throwers. It was over in less than two minutes.

The cops knew what the British bobbies have forgotten— that if you nip a riot in the bud, fewer people get hurt, and it's better for everyone. It is why in Paris, where I also once lived, the police break out the tear gas the minute they see a crowd getting out of hand—it demonstrates that the forces of law own the street, and it saves lives. I would not necessarily want a version of France's extremely aggressive and tough CRS [riot control force] in London—though arguably it is what Britain needs—but I cannot help thinking that if the patrolmen of Gotham's 9th precinct, with a few reinforcements, had been flown here on Sunday morning, they would have brought the whole thing to an end within hours.

On this the third day since the violence began, any racial and ethnic dimensions of the looting have yet to be parsed, at least in the mainstream media. From the footage it is clear that the rioters are mostly young and male—and that the mobs include plenty of white youths, though in some areas they seem to be disproportionately black.

On the other hand, members of Britain's South Asian and Muslim minorities seem to have played little or no part in the violence. On the contrary, large numbers of Muslim youths in the Bangladeshi-dominated sections of London's East End first guarded their mosques and then went to defend stores and banks from marauders.

In North London on the second day of the violence, Turkish and Kurdish storekeepers banded together, took up bats and broomsticks, and chased away would-be looters, despite being threatened with arrest by the police. (That is not a typo. The police were doing little or nothing to stop the looting, yet felt an urgent need to preserve their monopoly on the lawful use of force.) Though the victims were more diverse than the perpetrators, who tended to attack shopping areas in edgy, trendy mixed neighborhoods, it was striking that only immigrants seemed to show any serious inclination to defend their property and their livelihood. They were like L.A. Koreans, only without guns, a fact that made their courage even more remarkable.

As well as helping themselves to liquor and jewelry, the looters seemed to have a typically teenaged predilection for sportswear, mobile phones, and flat-screen TVs. However, they were also happy to smash up hairdressers, fast-food restaurants, and grocery stores.

Despite talk in the media and in left-wing circles about the riots being the result of public-sector cuts and unemployment (which is indeed high among Britain's undereducated youth), the rioters showed little compunction about destroying the workplaces of others. Moreover, the footage, much of it taken by the looters and their pals and then posted on the Web, showed little evidence of anger. Their mood seemed exuberant and excited—not unlike that of the students and sports fans who have recently rioted in North American cities after the local team wins or loses a major game.

None of the major commentators here in the United Kingdom seem to have heard of the sports-inspired riots in Vancouver and at Ohio State. They reflexively assume that anyone who sets cars on fire or smashes up a Starbucks must be motivated by anger or oppression. Perhaps because its members generally come from sheltered backgrounds, the British commentariat has little sense of the potential for violence, or the joy in disorder and aggression, to be found in most young men of military age. It is an odd thing, because I remember how, as Cambridge undergraduates, some of my friends and I did some dumb and destructive and illegal things—when we were confident that we would not be caught or that the price to be paid would be minimal.

Of course, there is a much more savage, bullying edge to this looting and vandalism than there was in my generation's drunken undergraduate pranks. And it is perhaps not altogether surprising that neither the police nor the public generally—with the exception of the tough Turks and Kurds—felt like taking on what were relatively small numbers of tough kids (seldom more than a couple of hundred). It is not just that many "hoodies" carry knives (this fact was cited as a reason for police caution by one of the ineffective cops the *London Times* quoted) and have no compunction in using them. They are accustomed to extreme, close-up, *Clockwork Orange*–style violence.

They are also accustomed to being given the free run of the streets. This is largely because Britain's police have, over the last two decades, adopted the hands-off, low-key, reactive model that American police departments disastrously moved to in the 1970s but then abandoned in the 1990s, most spectacularly in New York City. But in any case, the "hoodies" who this weekend demonstrated and reveled in their violent power like the gangsters in Walter Hill's classic 1979 movie *The Warriors* tend to be utterly unafraid of adults or any of the feeble sanctions offered by the adult world.

Britain's schools, laws, media, youth-worship, and policing have created what an angry Harlem preacher once called a "pediocracy"—literally a polity ruled by children, but here meaning one ruled by teenagers. As the world saw and the British public is having to acknowledge, it is not pretty. We can only be grateful that they don't have Kalashnikovs like their counterparts in such places as Somalia—yet.

A Toronto Program Tackles the Roots of Gang Violence

Maribel Gonzales

Maribel Gonzales (mgonzales@bell.net) is an international development consultant specializing in program development and management.

Toronto has witnessed several deadly outbreaks of gang violence that have prompted the city administration to search for solutions, Gonzales reports in the following viewpoint. Although youth violence is a complex issue with many contributing factors, one program—Breaking the Cycle (BTC)—has shown success. The goals of BTC are to keep at-risk youth out of gangs and to encourage those already in gangs to leave, Gonzales explains. The program focuses on identifying and addressing the risk factors for violent behavior and providing at-risk teens with opportunities for education and employment.

In 2011 Toronto, Canada's largest city (population c. 2.7 million), recorded its lowest murder count in 30 years—33. Then, this summer [2012] the city was rocked by brazen shootings that turned the Eaton Centre mall and a street block party into shooting galleries, leaving four dead and 28 injured. Gangs figure in both shootings. The alleged Eaton Centre shooter and two of the victims were affiliated with gangs while, according to the police, the block party shooting is connected to a leadership struggle in a gang.

Toronto Declares War on Gangs

The Toronto police track roughly 2,100 gang-involved or gang-associated individuals. Of these 500–600 are considered "really violent." Gangs have always existed in Toronto; the difference

Maribel Gonzales, "Breaking the Cycle of Gang Violence: A Toronto Program Aimed at Intervening with Youth Involved in Gang Activity Is Showing Results," *Ploughshares Monitor*, vol. 33, no. 3, Autumn 2012, p. 20. Copyright © 2012 by Project Ploughshares. All rights reserved. Reproduced by permission.

now is that gang violence more likely involves disenfranchised youth, occurs in public spaces, and uses high-powered guns.

The shootings sparked calls to curtail youth gang violence. Proposals spanned the political spectrum. Toronto Mayor [Rob] Ford declared a "war on thugs," echoing the federal government's tough-on-crime policies by calling for more cops and longer prison terms, and ridiculing "hug-a-thug" community programs. In contrast, city councillors called for social programs in identified "priority" neighbourhoods, some of which are scheduled to lose their funding in 2013. Ontario premier Dalton McGuinty cautioned against resorting to "simplistic" solutions.

No quick fix will curb gang-related gun violence. The problem is complex and each situation has its own underlying risk factors and dynamics. In Toronto, as in cities worldwide, most victims and perpetrators of gun violence are young males between the ages of 15 and 30 years. Indeed, responding to the problem of gangs and youth at risk of armed violence, especially in urban areas, has been identified as a global development programming gap. However, we lack knowledge about the outcomes and impacts of programs to combat youth violence. It is difficult to determine the effectiveness of interventions. What works? What needs to be changed?

Toronto Program Focuses on Encouraging Youth to Leave Gangs

In 2010 Project Ploughshares and Peacebuild conducted research on two programs—the Peace Management Initiative in Jamaica and the Breaking the Cycle (BTC) program in Toronto—aimed at intervening with youth who were involved or associated with gang activity. Ironically, a victim in the Eaton Centre shooting was trying to leave his gang past behind. Only a few months earlier he had signed up with BTC.

The BTC Gang Exit Strategy

BTC, which is a federally funded program run by the Canadian Training Institute (CTI), operates in two "priority" areas in Toronto known for gang activity. BTC's goal is to keep persons at risk out of gangs and to help those already in gangs leave. CTI found that the youth—most visible minorities and/or recent immigrants—faced multiple barriers to success. Most came from single or no-parent households; experienced home/community violence, guns, and racism; were not in school; abused drugs or alcohol; had arrest records; and had few employment opportunities.

BTC's premise is that youth can leave a violent lifestyle if individual circumstances that lead to antisocial, aggressive behaviours are addressed and barriers to education and employment are removed. It targets young men and women between the ages of 15 and 30 years, who are currently not in school, are unemployed, and have links with gangs, but who are committed to participating in BTC and accept cooperative group norms and agreements. The justice system, the police, social service agencies, schools, BTC graduates, and local parents refer participants to BTC.

Until recently, a BTC program cycle lasted 28 weeks and served 20–25 participants. Participants are paid a stipend equal to the Ontario minimum wage (currently $10.25 per hour) per 35-hour week. The provision of a stipend helps attract and keep participants, who learn money management skills and don't feel the need to turn to criminal activity for money.

In the past, BTC's program had four principal components, starting with six–eight hours of assessment to determine suitability and identify cognitive/behavioural and other issues that may need attention. Next came a two-week (70 hours) intensive personal development program to build trust; address violent behaviour, sexism, homophobia, and racism; and learn life skills that would allow the participants to build healthy relationships. Each participant charted an individual plan, including goals and activities to achieve them. (Because they have different needs, men and women have separate training curricula.) They then received a week of case management where progress was reviewed, and individual supportive guidance was provided on concerns such as housing, bank accounts, probation and court matters, and connecting to school and job opportunities. An additional 5–10 hours of miscellaneous support was provided per participant.

Participants then proceeded in one of three streams: 1) the Youth Ambassador Leadership Program, if they were deemed suitable, 2) discharge, or 3) referral to other agencies, such as an educational institution or a housing agency.

In the Youth Ambassador Leadership & Employment Program, participants received 25 weeks (875 hours) of further job readiness and personal development training, honed leadership skills, pursued community outreach activities, and made community presentations about BTC.

A Successful Program Struggles for Funding

Since 2003 BTC has helped approximately 350 clients. Eighty-eight per cent of participants have successfully graduated from BTC. Sixty-seven per cent of graduates are employed or are in school and not participating in gangs.

In 2008 the cost of BTC per participant was roughly $19,200 for approximately 1,000 hours of program intervention. While this is a significant investment, keeping an inmate incarcerated in a federal prison costs substantially more: $110,786 for males and $211,093 for females per year.

Most gang-involved youth are exposed to violence from childhood and may view violence as normal until they learn otherwise. Involving BTC graduates and youth ambassadors strengthens BTC's ability to reach out and involve neighbourhood youth and provides other youth with positive peer role models. When BTC participants return to school, get jobs, and participate in positive community activities, the cycle of gang violence is broken. This is especially important as many BTC participants are themselves parents.

A low attrition rate and generally positive outcomes can be traced to intensive individualized "treatment" tailored to the unique needs of participants. BTC successfully engages with its difficult cohort.

However, BTC is faced with unstable and inconsistent funding. Funds have to be raised for each program cycle, so BTC cannot consistently offer its services. Because of recent funding cuts only 14 rather than 25 clients can be served per cycle and for only 23 rather than 28 weeks. More critically, the program components have been significantly altered. Individual personal development has been reduced to five weeks in favour of placement in internships. Case management and support have also been reduced. The push is to get participants employed.

No complete evaluation of BTC has been done, despite a recommendation in a 2008 report commissioned by the federal government. So it is not clear why funds were cut and changes made to the BTC intervention strategy, which has been regarded as among the promising approaches in gang intervention.

When pressed for an explanation in a CBC interview (2012) CTI executive director John Sawdon stated:

> There is more and more pressure on not serving this group of people [gang-involved youth]. . . . The law and order agenda and tough-on-crime [perspective] was to say that those who have been gang-involved and engaging in criminal behaviour should be going to jail and we shouldn't be spending our money on them. The other piece is that if there were going to be programs, those programs should be linked to the workforce and not focused on personal development. The problem is the multiple barriers that you have

prevent people from entering the workforce to begin with and if you don't address those barriers they don't hold jobs.

These programming changes in BTC underscore the crucial need to invest in generating data and analysis so that policy and decision making are based on solid evidence about the outcomes, impacts, and effectiveness of programs.

Parks and Recreation Centers Are Offering a Positive Alternative to Gang Violence

Boris Weintraub

Boris Weintraub is a writer based in Washington, DC.

In the past, most cities responded to youth gang violence with law enforcement and prosecution, Weintraub contends in the following viewpoint. A more effective solution is to offer young people a positive alternative to gang activity, he maintains. Cities such as Los Angeles have begun programs centered around parks and recreation centers, providing a healthy outlet for young people's energy. In the first year of the Summer Night Lights program in Los Angeles, the city witnessed a 17 percent reduction in violent crimes.

Los Angeles is the epicenter of youth gang violence in the United States. Gangs infest big cities and small towns in all parts of the nation, but Los Angeles, with 40,000 members in 400 gangs, stands out—the "800-pound gorilla of gangs," in the words of one city official. For years, gang violence spiked in the hot summer months, especially at night. So in 2008, the city hit upon one of those simple ideas: Give young people something positive to do at night in the summer. Summer Night Lights was born.

Parks Provide a Positive Alternative

It wasn't all that simple, of course. A statistical analysis revealed that gang violence peaked in July and August, between 4 p.m. and midnight, from Wednesday to Saturday. The city

Boris Weintraub, "New Weapons in the Fight Against Gangs," *Parks & Recreation*, vol. 44, no. 11, November 2009, p. 46. Copyright © 2009 by National Recreation and Park Association. All rights reserved. Reproduced by permission.

chose eight neighborhoods with the highest crime rates, and kept their recreation centers open until midnight those four summer nights. It staffed each with 10 neighborhood residents aged 17 to 20 to help create programs and attract other at-risk youths, and inserted intervention workers to keep the peace and channel gang members into worthwhile activities. The centers offered free meals, sports, concerts, movies, discussions, mentoring, and a host of community-chosen programs to lure young people, keep them busy and happy, and even motivate them to change their ways.

That first year, the eight Summer Night Lights neighborhoods experienced a 17 percent drop in overall violent crime, including an astonishing 86 percent decrease in homicides and a 23 percent drop in aggravated assaults. In 2009, the program expanded to 15 recreation centers (and one school) and attracted nearly 50,000 visits a week for eight weeks, on a budget of $2.8 million, half from the city and the other half through philanthropic donations.

Los Angeles may have a bigger gang problem than any other U.S. city, and Summer Night Lights may be the most comprehensive of any city's efforts to fight gangs. But all over the nation, park and recreation departments are ramping up their fights in new and unusual ways. And like Los Angeles, most seek to engage gangbangers with positive programs, on their own turf, which often is the neighborhood park or recreation center.

Parks are a logical place to start, according to Los Angeles Department of Recreation and Parks general manager Jon Kirk Mukri.

"We're spread throughout the city, and we're neutral ground," Mukri says. "We welcome kids, we don't wear guns, we don't wear uniforms. Parks and recreation centers should be the crossroads of the community."

Mukri cites the neighborhood around Ramona Gardens, a housing project he calls "pretty dicey," whose older residents

In this photo, Eric Romero, also known as Lil Drawz, waits outside the gym at the Imperial Courts housing project. The gym and recreation center are taking part in the Summer Night Lights gang violence reduction program. © AP Images/Thomas Watkins.

would never have ventured outdoors a year ago. But last summer, the neighborhood recreation center offered free movies, and a lot of adults came out to see them. The program has been so successful that neighborhoods not included the first two years are asking to be included next year. Mayor Antonio Villaraigosa wants to be in 50 parks by 2013. "When people see the power of this program, there are no negatives," Mukri says.

At-Risk Kids Take Leadership Roles

The 10 local kids hired in each neighborhood are the key to the program's success, as well as the perfect example of how valuable it is to engage them, says Jeff Carr, formerly the city's deputy mayor for gang reduction and youth development and now the mayor's chief of staff. "We said to them, 'Every one of you, the story of your life is that you're a bad guy, a villain,'" Carr explains. "But we said, 'We're giving you the opportunity to write a new story, and you're going to be the heroes.' This is the easiest thing to convince people of—that this works."

In the past, most cities dealt with gangs by using "suppression," a fancy term for arrest. But in recent years, officials have concluded that if gang violence is to be dealt with, there have to be alternatives. As Mukri says, "We can't arrest our way out of this; we have to come up with something different." Other park and recreation leaders agree.

"You can always put a cop in a car and have him sit there," says Sue Black, director of Milwaukee County Parks, which includes the city and surrounding areas. "But you have to get kids into positive programs. If they plant a tree, they're vested in that tree and won't vandalize it."

Black means that literally. One of her department's programs is a partnership with Urban Ecology Center, which reaches out to Milwaukee's children and adults to teach them about the natural world. It uses the county's parks and waterways as classrooms, with courses in native plants, kayaking, canoeing, and wildlife. "I want lots of these centers in our parks in 10 years," she says. "I want the urban ecology centers to be a combination of nature center and ecology teaching center for our kids."

The Milwaukee system, like its counterparts everywhere, has limited funds and staff, so, says Black, "I'll partner with everybody." She has joined forces with the Boys & Girls Clubs [of America], a golf program for city kids called First Tee, a tennis program, a year-round camp for inner city kids. She's especially proud of her system's success in turning Bradford Beach, a Lake Michigan landmark that had fallen on hard times, into a Blue Wave beach that is so filled with activities of all kinds that something is always going on and gangs that had made it their turf now stay away.

Ask Black what age group she tries to target, and she answers quickly: "All of them. When they're 24, they're still kids to me." The Urban Ecology Center begins with kindergartners, for example, but runs all the way through elementary school, and high school kids can get jobs in the park system through a tie with AmeriCorps. If she had her way, there would always be activities for everyone.

"My philosophy is displacement," she says. "There are areas the gangs have established as theirs. But if I can get a group in with positive activities, they can't stop a facility from functioning for its intended purpose."

"A Busy Park Is a Safe Park"

Most cities trying to reduce gang violence deny that they specifically target at-risk kids. As Nanette Smejkal, director of El Paso's parks and recreation department, says, "From our perspective, all kids are at risk. That's why they need positive programs."

Take Denver, for example. It has no activities that overtly aim at the city's 80 gangs, with an estimated 6,000 members. But Denver's parks and recreation department offers numerous alternatives. Kids Prime Time brings youngsters ages 7 to 15 into recreation centers between 6 and 9 p.m. for music, dance, games, and crafts. Year-round after-school programs provide extra help with homework, mentoring, encouragement in keeping out of trouble, and—a crucial element for many in poor neighborhoods in Denver and elsewhere—a snack. And then there is Hoopin' with Hickenlooper, a summer basketball program for kids 7 to 15 honoring mayor John Hickenlooper.

In 2008, the city provided free access during the summer to all its recreation centers and parks for kids under the age of 17, waiving the annual membership fee that proved onerous for many poorer youngsters. Jill McGranahan, the department's communications director, says Denver police reported a 30 percent drop in youth crime, including violent crime, that summer; funding from the Kaiser Family Foundation permitted free access again in the summer of 2009.

Denver's expanded offerings to youths began after a task force examined how the city was fighting gangs, mostly through suppression. "We realized we couldn't sustain the model we had," McGranahan says. One task force member was Francisco Gallardo, program director for Gang Rescue and Support Project (GRASP), a local anti-gang group. Gallardo brought a special expertise to the task force: He himself was a former gang member.

"A lot of gangs hang around the local rec center, they see it as their property. So what do you do to turn that around?" he asks. He lauds free summer access, but adds: "What about lunch? If schools can provide free lunch during the school year, why can't the parks?" And he notes that the park system must offer activities that reflect the community.

"If you have a Mexican neighborhood, you want to have soccer, because that appeals to them, but some parks don't even have a soccer field," he says. "I used to run arts programs in Mexican centers, and we'd have painting on wood, tinwork, things that are culturally relevant the kids can identify with. Sometimes kids go to a rec center but just hang around outside. You want the center to be a support group that can attract them and bring them inside."

Gallardo, 37, recalls the people who helped him turn his life around when, at the age of 19, he faced prison time and was involved in gang violence.

"The first major intervention in my life was from a rec center basketball coach," he says. "He'd come around, wake me up, make sure I got to practice. He didn't give up on me. It was direct intervention."

Now he is on the other side, trying to redirect the lives of gang members in the Denver area. "We try to motivate them to engage in pro-social behavior," he says. "We try to plant the seeds and hope they germinate."

Dealing with Gangs Around the Country

The city council of Orem, Utah, faced with a rising problem of gang violence and graffiti, recently declared the city's parks and public schools off-limits to gang members, who can be ordered off the grounds by police and arrested if they return. Which is, of course, one way of dealing with gangs. Here are some other strategies adopted by park and recreation departments around the country:

- Philadelphia's department of recreation, recognizing that most "negative behavior" and violence takes place after school hours, invites youths into 100 recreation centers between 3 and 6 p.m. Monday through Friday. The youngsters receive homework assistance, play games, participate in sports and arts programming, and receive healthy snacks. This year, it serves 2,800 youngsters.

- Houston has adopted an active anti-graffiti program for the city's 350 parks. A playground and park inspection group works with a graffiti abatement contractor and tries to respond to information about gang graffiti within 24 hours of learning about it.

- Houston also operates a summer program that provides free, nutritious lunches in recreation centers to young people under the age of 18 Monday through Friday, and adds a healthy snack between 3 and 4 p.m.

- Pittsburgh's department of parks and recreation offers free, healthy hot meals, family style, to youngsters from kindergarten age to 18 between 5 and 7 p.m. Monday through Friday year-round, in the hopes of improving nutrition and keeping them productively engaged.

- The Austin, Texas, parks and recreation department's Neighborhood Teen Program invites teenagers to come to recreation centers to bowl, do cleanup work, and discuss ways to avoid gang participation and substance abuse in a structured environment.

- Durham, North Carolina, launched a "Campaign4Change" in its parks and recreation department that included a two-hour anti-gang play written by a former gang member. The campaign was designed to change the mind-set of gang members, and included poems, music, and entertainment during spring break.

- Dallas's juvenile gang prevention program, started in 1991, stresses "positive pathways for at-risk youth" in four recreation centers. The program features classes devoted to theater and to the visual arts, and had participants create their own plays based on personal experience.

- El Paso's parks and recreation department offers after-school programs, evening sessions, teaching, mentoring, sports and "whatever else the kids themselves say they want," says director Nanette Smejkal. The city uses funds from a five-year federal grant to the police department for recreation programs in its 200 parks and 15 recreation centers.

Violence Against Women Is a Human Rights Issue

Latin American and Caribbean Women's Health Network

Women's Health Journal *is a publication of the Latin American and Caribbean Women's Health Network.*

There is no excuse for violence against women, argue the editors of Women's Health Journal *in the following viewpoint. They cite research stating that 60 percent of all women globally have been the victim of physical violence at least once in their lives. Much progress has been made in recent years to raise awareness of this serious issue, the editors report.*

Violence against women and girls is a phenomenon with the characteristics of a pandemic, due to the scope and magnitude of this violence in our societies and the high impact that it has on the lives and health of the women affected, their families and communities. There is no country that is completely free of this scourge.

There Are No Excuses for Violence Against Women

Now more than ever, there is a need for broad mobilization by civil society to urge the eradication of these violent behaviors that are expressed in all areas, both private and public, and also to demand severe punishment for the men who engage in them. However, the most urgent need is to deconstruct the social structures that permit the power of male domination and the continued subordination of women. This abominable discrimination lies at the root of all expressions of gender-based violence for it continues to maintain that women are inferior to men and that it is perfectly acceptable to discipline women and girls with beatings, threats or coercion.

But nothing justifies violence against women and girls. Neither should we look for explanations of possible pathologies in the aggressors or personal characteristics of the victims that make them more prone to abuse. Factors such as poverty, unemployment and alcoholism are no excuse either. States, meanwhile, cannot escape their responsibility in prevention and punishment of violence and care and compensation for the victims.

In recent decades, organized action against gender-based violence has made remarkable progress, especially in getting this item put on the agenda of United Nations [UN] conferences like the World Conference on Human Rights in Vienna (1993) and the World Conference on Women in Beijing (1995), with their respective follow-ups. The International Conference on Population and Development in Cairo, the World [Summit for] Social Development in Copenhagen, the World Conference Against Racism (Durban, 2001) and other conferences on the status of women also addressed this issue with particular relevance.

Similarly, in terms of the human rights protection system, today there are treaties, conventions and declarations that address violence against women and girls as an issue of human rights and discrimination, such as the Convention on the Elimination of All Forms of Discrimination Against Women (CEDAW), the UN Declaration on the Elimination of Violence Against Women, the [Inter-American] Convention on the Prevention, Punishment and Eradication of Violence Against Women (Convention of Belem do Para) and the Rome statute that created the International Criminal Court. The UN has also appointed a special rapporteur on violence against women, its causes and consequences, with a mandate that has allowed this UN official to receive complaints and initiate investigations on violence against women in all United Nations member states.

The Women's Movement Has Raised Awareness

For its part, the women's movement against violence has been at the forefront in recent decades to reverse the situation, acting on several levels: lobbying the government and other sectors with decision-making power to demand responses in terms of laws, policies and programs consistent with this dramatic reality. At the same time, the movement has undertaken public actions on symbolic dates promoting campaigns to raise awareness, provide information and denounce gender-based violence. One of these efforts, probably the most widespread initiative throughout the world, is the campaign commemorating November 25, International Day [for the Elimination of] Violence Against Women, which also has been incorporated into the work of the United Nations and has been taken up by some governments that are sensitive to this issue.

Since 1996, the Latin American and Caribbean Women's Health Network [LACWHN] has coordinated a regional campaign, with various calls for action, that seeks to expose the tragic consequences of gender-based violence in the lives of women and girls and to draw attention to the comprehensive health impacts of this violence. This year's call for action was "End Violence Against Women! Stop the Damage, Discrimination and Death!" and it had the following main objective:

- To foster and demand a greater social commitment from the states to prevent, punish and eradicate violence against women and girls, defending their full human rights and promoting and protecting their comprehensive health.

As specific objectives, the call for action proposed to:

- Promote advocacy and participation in policy making with state actors to demand public policies and legislation that protect women's right to live healthy lives free from gender-based violence.

- Open dialogue and reflection within communities to help eliminate the normalization of violence against women, raising awareness that gender-based violence is a violation of women's human rights and an expression of discrimination that has affected women for millennia.

At the same time, LACWHN coordinates the Campana Punto Final hacia la Violencia contra las Mujeres (Campaign to End Violence Against Women) in Latin America and the Caribbean, with a first stage taking place in Brazil, Bolivia, Haiti and Guatemala. . . . The campaign is also a concrete contribution to the United Nations' worldwide campaign, UNiTE to End Violence Against Women, which the United Nations secretary-general launched in 2008 to coordinate international efforts to address this phenomenon.

Violence Against Women Is Widespread

Gender-based violence can affect any woman, regardless of age, socioeconomic status, place of residence, type of work, race/ethnicity, sexual preference, educational level, religious belief or other status. Today, violence is a latent risk in the lives of all women and girls, who may even die as a result. The most extreme form of gender-based violence—femicide—unfortunately continues to increase.

Only when the universal culture of the 21st century incorporates and validates a new relationship between women and men based on respect, peace, equality and justice, will we achieve the effective eradication of all violations of women's human rights.

During a visit to Mexico on November 25, 2010, the United Nations High Commissioner for Human Rights (OHCHR), Navi Pillay, spoke out regarding a recent finding that 60% of women worldwide have been subjected to physical violence at least once in their lives. "No nation, rich or poor, whether a dictatorship or a democracy, has come close to eliminating violence against women," Pillay declared, warning that such figures are important because they are a reminder of the problem's prevalence, but they may eventually numb us to the harsh reality that behind every number, there is an act of violence that hurts a girl or a woman.

For Further Discussion

1. In chapter 1, Geoffrey Aggeler describes music as a major influence on Burgess. Unable to major in music at university because of a poor grade on a physics exam, the writer studied English literature. The relationship between literature and music was a recurrent theme in his works, the critic explains. Explain the role of music in *A Clockwork Orange*.

2. In chapter 2, Thomas Reed Whissen writes that *A Clockwork Orange* was well received by the youth of the 1960s and 1970s who were rebelling against their parents' generation. In what ways is the novel relevant to today's teenagers, and in what ways is it dated?

3. In chapter 2, critics Bernard Bergonzi and Geoffrey Aggeler interpret the message of *A Clockwork Orange* in different ways. Bergonzi suggests that Burgess has a pessimistic view of human nature, believing that people choose evil of their own free will because they find it enjoyable, and not because of social conditioning. Aggeler contends that Burgess has a more positive view of human nature, arguing that by turning away from violence, Alex is demonstrating that people can learn from their mistakes and repent. With which critic do you agree? Use examples from the novel to support your position.

4. In chapter 2, Deanna Madden writes that the violence against women in *A Clockwork Orange* is troubling because Burgess seems to condone it with his message that even a life of evil and violence is preferable to a life with no choice. She points out that women are presented as inferior to men and suggests that the author may share

Alex's distain for women. Do you find the violence against women in the novel more disturbing than the other violence? What are your reasons?

5. In chapter 3, William R. Brownfield, Maribel Gonzales, and Boris Weintraub write that youth can be kept out of violent gangs by offering them more positive alternatives, such as education, employment, and recreation. Do you think any of these alternatives would be attractive to Alex and his gang members? Why, or why not?

6. In chapter 3, Jonathan Foreman is critical of the low-key reaction of London police to youth gang violence in the summer of 2011. A more aggressive response to violence is needed, he contends, or the country will be at the mercy of lawless teenagers. Foreman says the violence is reminiscent of that described in *A Clockwork Orange*. Do you think that Burgess would agree that more forceful policing is an answer to violence? Why, or why not?

For Further Reading

Ray Bradbury, *Fahrenheit 451*. New York: Ballantine, 1953.

Anthony Burgess, *Earthly Powers*. New York: Simon & Schuster, 1980.

————, *The Wanting Seed*. London: Heinemann, 1962.

William S. Burroughs, *Naked Lunch*. Paris: Olympia Press, 1959; New York: Grove, 1962.

William Golding, *Lord of the Flies*. London: Faber, 1954.

Joseph Heller, *Catch-22*. New York: Simon & Schuster, 1961.

Aldous Huxley, *Brave New World*. New York: Doubleday, 1932.

Ken Kesey, *One Flew over the Cuckoo's Nest*. New York: Viking, 1962.

George Orwell, *Animal Farm*. London: Secker & Warburg, 1945.

————, *Nineteen Eighty-Four*. London: Secker & Warburg, 1949.

B.F. Skinner, *Walden Two*. New York: Macmillan, 1948.

Kurt Vonnegut Jr., *Slaughterhouse-Five; or, The Children's Crusade: A Duty-Dance with Death*. New York: Delacorte, 1969.

Yevgeny Zamyatin, *We*. New York: E.P. Dutton, 1924.

Bibliography

Books

Geoffrey Aggeler, ed.	*Critical Essays on Anthony Burgess.* Boston: G.K. Hall, 1986.
Andrew Biswell	*The Real Life of Anthony Burgess.* London: Picador, 2005.
Samuel Coale	*Anthony Burgess.* New York: Frederick Ungar Co., 1981.
Walter S. DeKeseredy	*Violence Against Women: Myths, Facts, Controversies.* Toronto: University of Toronto Press, 2011.
Rona M. Fields	*Against Violence Against Women: The Case for Gender as a Protected Class.* New York: Palgrave Macmillan, 2013.
Earl G. Ingersoll and Mary C. Ingersoll, eds.	*Conversations with Anthony Burgess.* Jackson: University Press of Mississippi, 2008.
Peter Krämer	*A Clockwork Orange: Controversies.* New York: Palgrave Macmillan, 2011.
Jorja Leap	*Jumped In: What Gangs Taught Me About Violence, Drugs, Love, and Redemption.* Boston, MA: Beacon Press, 2012.
Roger Lewis	*Anthony Burgess.* New York: Thomas Dunne, 2004.

Paul Phillips   *A Clockwork Counterpoint: The Music and Literature of Anthony Burgess.* Manchester, UK: Manchester University Press, 2010.

Alan R. Roughley, ed.   *Anthony Burgess and Modernity.* Manchester, UK: Manchester University Press, 2008.

John W. Tilton   *Cosmic Satire in the Contemporary Novel.* Lewisburg, PA: Bucknell University Press, 1977.

Periodicals

Carl C. Bell   "Teen Gangs: Integrated Interventions Work Best," *Clinical Psychiatry News*, October 2010.

Anthony Burgess   "Alex on Today's Youth: Creeching Golosses and Filthy Toofles!," *New York Times Book Review*, May 31, 1987.

Wayne C. Connelly   "Optimism in Burgess's *A Clockwork Orange*," *Extrapolation*, December 1972.

John Cullinan   "Anthony Burgess: The Art of Fiction," *Paris Review*, Spring 1973.

John Cullinan   "Anthony Burgess' *A Clockwork Orange*: Two Versions," *English Language Notes*, June 1972.

Todd F. Davis and Kenneth Womack	"'O My Brothers': Reading the Anti-Ethics of the Pseudo-Family in Anthony Burgess's *A Clockwork Orange*," *College Literature*, Spring 2002.
Carol Dix	"An Interview with Anthony Burgess," *Transatlantic Review*, Spring–Summer 1972.
National Gang Center Quarterly Newsletter	"Talking to Youth About Gangs," Spring 2013. http://corrections .com/news/article/33440/talkinq -to-youth-about-gangs.
Kate O'Brien et al	"Youth Gang Affiliation, Violence, and Criminal Activities: A Review of Motivational, Risk, and Protective Factors," *Aggression and Violent Behavior*, July–August 2013.
William H. Pritchard	"The Novels of Anthony Burgess," *Massachusetts Review*, Summer 1966.
Rubin Rabinovitz	"Ethical Values in Anthony Burgess's *Clockwork Orange*," *Studies in the Novel*, Spring 1979.
Philip E. Ray	"Alex Before and After: A New Approach to Burgess's *A Clockwork Orange*," *Modern Fiction Studies*, Autumn 1981.

Chris Smith   "On the Block: A Pilot Program in
                           Oakland, California, Combines
                           Community Policing with Social
                           Services and Gets At-Risk Young Men
                           off the Street," *American Prospect*,
                           January–February 2011.

Walter Sullivan   "Death Without Tears: Anthony
                           Burgess and the Dissolution of the
                           West," *Hollins Critic*, April 1969.

Michael W.   "Toy Soldiers and America's Killing
Waters   Fields," *Black Voices—Huffington Post*,
                           July 18, 2013.

Index

human rights issue, 172–176
scope, 172, 175–176
Violence and language. *See* Language
Violence in media
Burgess' questions and critique, 57–60, 68
literature structure, 93
A Vision of Battlements (novel), 22, 24, 37, 95
Vonnegut, Kurt, 91

W

Walden Two (Skinner), 101, 135
The Wanting Seed (novel), 17, 29, 71, 77, 93, 94, 102, 103, 107
Waugh, Evelyn, 78, 79, 84, 97
We (Zamyatin), 93
Weintraub, Boris, 164–171
Westerns, 91
Whissen, Thomas Reed, 85–92
Wilson, John Anthony Burgess. *See* Burgess, Anthony
Women
Alex's hostility, 111–116, 134
Burgess' hostility, 111, 116–117, 118
gang members, 140
language and gender, 111–112, 134

physical features and objectification, 81, 97, 111–112, *113*, 115–116, 117, 118–119
violence against as human rights issue, 172–176
Women's movement, 174–175
The Worm and the Ring (novel), 11, 17, 25, 29, 37
Writing processes
Burgess' creativity and methods, 12–14, 22–23, 25, 27, 32–33, 37–39, 44–46, 47–48, 95, 124–125
A Clockwork Orange motif, 52–53, 66, 127

X

X-rated films, 90

Y

Youth Alive! (gang violence prevention program), 141–142
Youth rebellion and violence, 86–87, 88–91, 93, 104. *See also* Gangs
You've Had Your Time (memoir), 19, 35

Z

Zamyatin, Yevgeny, 93, 94–95

CPSIA information can be obtained
at www.ICGtesting.com
Printed in the USA
FFOW03n1055250316
22647FF

3830252